HEALTHY HEART COOKBOOK

Cod Stewed with Onions, Potatoes, Corn, and Tomatoes, page 108.

HEALTHY HEART COOKBOOK

WITH AN INTRODUCTION BY **Robyn Webb, M.S., L.N.**

FOOD PHOTOGRAPHY BY **Renée Comet**

Oxmoor House®

Oxmoor House®

ISBN: 0-8487-2766-5
Printed in the U.S.A.
10 9 8 7 6 5 4 3 2 1

Healthy Heart Cookbook

Vice President and Publisher: **Neil Levin**
Senior Director of Acquisitions and Editorial Resources:
Jennifer Pearce
Director of New Product Development:
Carolyn M. Clark
Director of Marketing: **Inger Forland**
Director of Trade Sales: **Dana Hobson**
Director of Custom Publishing: **John Lalor**
Director of Special Markets: **Robert Lombardi**
Director of Design: **Kate L. McConnell**

Project Editor: **Ruth Goldberg**
Technical Specialist: **Monika Lynde**
Production Manager: **Vanessa Hunnibell**
Quality Assurance: **Jim King, Stacy L. Eddy**

Design: **Studio A, Alexandria, Virginia**
Photography: **Renée Comet Photography, Inc.**
Food Styling: **Lisa Cherkasky**
Nutritional Analysis: **Hill Nutrition Associates**

Special Contributors: **Ellen Calloway** (photo assistance);
Arlene Soodak (props coordination); **Jody Billert** (design
assistance); **Teresa Graham** (text coordination); **Susan
Deresckey** (recipe editing); **Elizabeth Hiser, R.D.**
(introduction); **Christine Ryan Spengler, R.D.** (nutrition
notes); **Jane Harvey** (copyediting); **Celia Beattie** (proof-
reading); **Rose Grant** (index).

Props: The editors wish to thank the following individuals
and companies: Apartment Zero, Washington, D.C.;
Appalachian Spring, Washington, D.C.; Chris Simoncelli,
Atlanta, Georgia; Coffee and The Works, Washington, D.C.;
Dean & Deluca, Washington, D.C.; French Country Living,
Great Falls, Virginia.; LA DE DA, Potomac, Maryland;
Leslye Fenton, Washington, D.C.; Mikasa, Rockville,
Maryland; Moss & Co., Washington, D.C.; Pottery Barn,
Kensington, Maryland; Simon Pearce, Bethesda,
Maryland; Simply Home, Washington, D.C.; Smith &
Hawken, Washington, D.C.; Teaism, Washington, D.C.;
Williams-Sonoma, Washington, D.C.

Recipe shown on facing page: Watermelon Sorbet,
page 140.

CONTENTS

INTRODUCTION

VITAMINS

FIBER

ANTIOXIDANTS

Eating for Heart Health

It's our pleasure to bring you the good news: Eating for a healthy heart no longer means having to deprive yourself. And the recipes you'll find in the *Healthy Heart Cookbook* prove the point. From simple, nutritious breakfasts to hearty, delicious dinners, **you'll be doing the right thing** for your heart — and your taste buds — with every recipe in this book. They're all based on the new heart-healthy "diet," which is **abundant in tasty, whole foods** that both protect and truly satisfy. Instead of making you worry about what *not* to eat, the new way of thinking invites you to eat **a rich, varied diet** by focusing on the healing ingredients in many foods.

Let's start with one of the biggest changes in heart-healthy eating: Extreme low-fat diets are out. It's now clear that **there are good, safe fats** that don't contribute to heart disease risk and that tool little fat may even be dangerous. You'll still need to **limit saturated fats** — the type found in fatty meats and full-fat dairy products — and cut back on the hydrogenated fats found in baked goods, crackers, fried foods, and some types of margarine; hydrogenation creates trans-fatty acids (or trans fats), which can be as detrimental as saturated fats. But there are at least three reasons why many authorities no longer suggest severe restriction of all fats to guard against heart disease:

- **When you force fat in the diet to very low levels, you tend to eat more carbohydrates.** In many people, high carbohydrate intake raises triglyceride levels, and high triglycerides recently have been identified as a risk factor for heart disease.

- **Low-fat/high carbohydrate diets tend to lower HDL, the "good" cholesterol** that offers powerful protection against heart disease.

- **Recent studies show that low-fat diets may worsen the cholesterol picture** further by transforming the "bad" LDL cholesterol into a small, dense form that could be even more damaging to arteries.

Good fats are in. The trick is to make sure that any fat you add to foods is monounsaturated—mainly olive or canola oils—and to keep an eye on your overall calorie count: Obesity is still a major risk factor for heart disease. Monounsaturated fats don't raise LDL as do saturated and hydrogenated fats, nor do they raise triglycerides or blood sugar as carbohydrates tend to do. And they don't lower HDL as polyunsaturated fats do. This is great news for those of us who love to cook and eat, because there is nothing like a little fat to deliver the full flavor of food.

Love those omega-3s. Omega-3 fatty acids, the type of fats found in fish, have long been known to be good for heart health. They offer protection not by lowering cholesterol, it turns out, but by warding off irregular heartbeats and blood clots that can precipitate a heart attack. They also tend to lower the body's inflammatory response—good news, since inflammation of artery walls contributes to atherosclerosis. This is critical if you have already suffered a heart attack or have been diagnosed with heart disease. Studies suggest that eating a weekly meal of a fatty fish like salmon supplies enough omega-3s to reduce certain types of heart attacks by 40 percent.

Eat more foods from plant sources. Study after study has shown the benefits of eating lots of fruits, vegetables, and whole grains, which appear to protect against heart disease and cancer. But you don't need to give up meat. Just bring plant foods to the center of the plate. You can use smaller amounts of lean meat as flavoring for vegetable, bean, and grain dishes and save that roast for a special occasion. Soy products, beans, and other legumes have been shown to lower cholesterol—particularly when added to a diet that's already rich in heart-healthy foods—and they are a great alternative to meat-based dishes.

The multicolored dream plate. The next time you find yourself wondering what to eat, think color. The incredible range of hues you see in the produce aisle is more than just attractive packaging. Plant foods contain a rich store of naturally occurring substances called phytochemicals that protect plant cells; when we eat them they protect us too. For example, the red, orange, and yellow pigments in the carotenoid family act as antioxidants, protecting cells from the wear and tear of everyday living; tomatoes, yellow bell peppers, carrots, and purple cabbage are good sources. The red and purple colors found in the skins of grapes and apples come from the flavonoid family and behave similarly. Carotenoids and flavonoids are only two of the dozens of phytochemical families that have been identified so far. A general rule of thumb: The richer the color, the richer the store of phytochemicals.

High blood pressure? Accentuate the positive. Even if you have high blood pressure, you probably don't need to throw away your salt shaker. First of all, more than 90 percent of the sodium in a typical diet comes from processed foods, not the salt people add at the table. Even more important, a large body of research suggests that for most Americans, sodium has little to do with high blood pressure. As few as 15 percent of us have an inherited tendency toward sodium sensitivity; and even for this group, there are better strategies for keeping blood pressure down than simply slashing salt. First, keep overall body weight in check: More body tissue requires more vessels to supply with blood, forcing the heart to work harder. Second, eating 7 to 10 servings of fruits and vegetables a day and 2 to 3 servings of low-fat dairy products has been shown to lower blood pressure effectively; the benefit rises when sodium is kept at or below recommended levels. Researchers suspect that a rich supply of the minerals potassium, magnesium, and calcium contained in fruits, vegetables, and low-fat dairy products are just as important in lowering blood pressure as cutting back on sodium.

Fill up on fiber. If you want to enjoy foods that are low in calories, more satisfying, and more protective, choose the ones you can eat just as you find them. Vegetables, grains, and fruits in their natural state contain fiber—parts of the plant that are virtually calorie-free because we can't digest them. Fiber slows down your eating because it makes you chew

longer, holds many times its weight in water, and fills you up. The result: Fiber helps limit the number of calories you take in. Dietary fiber is either soluble or insoluble. Soluble fiber helps lower blood cholesterol and slows the digestion of carbohydrates. Oats, whole-grain rye, and beans are the richest sources of soluble fiber. Insoluble fiber—the type that predominates in whole wheat and other grains—also may play a role in preventing heart disease.

Beyond cholesterol. Although we still need to maintain blood cholesterol at healthful levels, new research suggests that we also should keep an eye on homocysteine, another substance in the blood that has been linked to heart disease. Normally homocysteine, an amino acid, remains at low levels because it is steadily converted into another amino acid used to make proteins. This conversion is directed by the B vitamin folate (folic acid). When the body doesn't have enough folate, homocysteine levels build up in the blood and contribute to artery damage. This finding helped inspire the government to fortify foods with folic acid, but surveys suggest that most Americans still aren't getting enough. The solution? Choose leafy greens and beans or fortified foods like pasta or whole-grain cereals and breads. And take a daily multivitamin supplement to be certain you're getting enough folate. Multivitamins also contain vitamins B_{12} and B_6, which assist folate in doing a complete job of keeping homocysteine at safe levels.

NOTE *Unless you know you are iron deficient, it's best to take a supplement without iron. Too much iron can cause heart damage in some people.*

A new way of living. It's time to start thinking of "diet" in terms of the original meaning of the word: *a way of living.* We hope the recipes in this book, based on all of the principles outlined above, can help you begin a new way of living that results in abundant good health. Use it as a guide, add your own creativity, and enjoy the pleasures of eating well!

How to use our nutritional analyses: The numbers that accompany each recipe represent the nutrients found in a single serving of the finished product. Keep in mind that 1 gram of protein = 4 calories, 1 gram of fat = 9 calories, and 1 gram of carbohydrate = 4 calories. You can determine your daily requirements of nutritional elements from the following information.

- **Calories:** To maintain your current weight, you need a daily supply of roughly 12 to 15 calories per pound of body weight, depending on your level of activity. For example, if you weigh 135 pounds and are quite active, multiply 135 x 15 calories for a total of 2,025 calories per day.

- **Fat:** It's still a smart idea to pursue the goal of getting no more than 30 percent of your calories from fat, as recommended by the American Heart Association and many other health agencies. To estimate how many total grams of fat you should aim for, multiply your daily calorie level by 30 percent and then divide the product by 9. For example, if you need 2,000 calories per day: 2,000 calories x .3 = 600 calories / 9 calories per gram of fat = 67 grams.

- **Saturated Fat:** The American Heart Association recommends that you get no more than 10 percent of your calories from saturated fat, which works out to about 22 grams of saturated fat per day in the example above. However, keep in mind that for the best protection, you want to restrict saturated fat as much as possible.

- **Carbohydrates:** A gram of carbohydrate contains 4 calories. About 50 to 60 percent of your daily calories should come from carbohydrates, which translates to 250 to 300 grams in our example of a 2,000-calorie diet. If you have high triglyceride levels, you'll do better to aim for the lower end of the carbohydrate range.

- **Protein:** Adults need about .4 gram of protein per pound of body weight a day to stay healthy, or about 60 grams per day for a 150-pound person. Ideally, as much of that as possible should come from plant sources, such as beans, soy products, and other legumes.

- **Cholesterol:** The recommended limit is 300 milligrams of dietary cholesterol per day. But keep in mind that dietary cholesterol levels don't translate directly to *blood cholesterol* levels. In actuality, saturated fat raises blood cholesterol levels more than dietary cholesterol does.

- **Sodium:** The current recommended limit is 2,400 milligrams of sodium a day, roughly the amount found in a teaspoon of salt.

- **Fiber:** Adults are advised to eat at least 25 to 35 grams of dietary fiber a day for good health. Many of us currently get less than half that amount. Breakfast is a great fiber opportunity—whole-grain or bran cereals and fruit are excellent sources. And if you find you need a snack during the day, use it as a chance to meet your fiber quota by eating fruits, vegetables, and whole grains.

GOOD FAT FACTS

Of the monounsaturates, olive oil is best for sautéing, oven frying, or grilling while canola oil is ideal for baking. Oils oxidize (go rancid) easily; avoid this by using glass rather than plastic containers and by storing oils in a cupboard, away from light and heat. When it comes to omega-3s, your best bets are salmon, mackerel, albacore tuna, and fresh sardines, but there are good plant sources, too. The best of these are flaxseed products, canola oil, walnuts, leafy greens, and soybean products.

HEALTHY STARTS

PEACH SMOOTHIE

1 In a blender, process the peaches, yogurt, tofu, orange juice, and honey or sugar until smooth. With the blender on, add the ice cubes one at a time and process until smooth.

HEALTH NOTE | *This smoothie is a delicious way to incorporate cholesterol-lowering soy protein into your diet. Tofu and other soy foods have been shown to fight heart disease. Drink this smoothie for breakfast or as an afternoon pick-me-up.*

SERVES: 4

3 cups sliced fresh peaches

1 cup vanilla nonfat yogurt

¾ cup (about 4 oz.) cubed silken tofu, drained

½ cup orange juice

3 tbsp. honey or sugar

5 ice cubes

CALORIES: **182**   FAT: **1 G**   SAT. FAT: **0 G**   CARBOHYDRATES: **41 G**   PROTEIN: **6 G**   CHOLESTEROL: **2 MG**   SODIUM: **43 MG**   FIBER: **2 G**

APRICOT-MANGO SMOOTHIE

1 Combine all the ingredients in a blender and whip until smooth.

HEALTH NOTE | *This tropical drink is loaded with the antioxidant beta carotene. In addition to fighting heart disease, antioxidants help protect against cancer.*

SERVES: 2

1 cup apricot nectar

½ cup diced fresh apricots, unpeeled

½ cup diced fresh mango, frozen at least 30 minutes

½ fresh banana, sliced and frozen

½ cup plain nonfat yogurt

CALORIES: **174**   FAT: **.6 G**   SAT. FAT: **.2 G**   CARBOHYDRATES: **40 G**   PROTEIN: **5 G**   CHOLESTEROL: **1 MG**   SODIUM: **48 MG**   FIBER: **2 G**

MAKES ABOUT 16 SERVINGS

1 cup unsweetened puffed wheat

1 cup unsweetened puffed rice

1 cup unsweetened puffed corn

1 cup rolled oats

1 cup bran flakes

1 cup puffed millet or millet flakes

½ cup seedless raisins or currants

2 tbsp. chopped toasted almonds, hazelnuts, or pecans

1 Combine the cereals in a large bowl. Stir in the raisins or currants and the nuts. Store the cereal mix in an airtight container.

HEALTH NOTE | *This cereal mix is a heart-healthy alternative to granolas, which can be outrageously high in calories. You can find puffed or flaked whole grains at most health food stores.*

CALORIES: **61**   FAT: **1 G**   SAT. FAT: **0 G**   CARBOHYDRATES: **12 G**   PROTEIN: **2 G**   CHOLESTEROL: **0 MG**   SODIUM: **24 MG**   FIBER: **1 G**

GRAIN

NUTS

RAISINS

SERVES: 6

1 red apple, coarsely chopped

1 yellow apple, coarsely chopped

½ cup apple cider or unsweetened apple juice

1 cup quick-cooking rolled oats

1 tbsp. honey

1 cup plain low-fat yogurt

2 tbsp. sliced almonds

2 tbsp. raisins

Dark brown sugar, for sprinkling

1 Put the apples into a large bowl. Add the cider or apple juice and toss the apples to moisten them. Stir in the oats and honey, then add the yogurt, almonds, and raisins. Stir to combine the mixture well.

2 Serve the oatmeal in individual bowls; sprinkle each serving with ½ teaspoon of the brown sugar.

TIP | *If you like oatmeal, try preparing high-fiber oat bran as a hot cereal. It cooks up quickly and has a smoother, creamier texture.*

CALORIES: 152   FAT: 3 G   SAT. FAT: .6 G   CARBOHYDRATES: 29 G   PROTEIN: 5 G   CHOLESTEROL: 2 MG   SODIUM: 29 MG   FIBER: 3 G

1 Combine the orange juice, orange zest, and banana in a nonreactive saucepan and bring the mixture to a boil. Stir in the oats, reduce the heat to low, and cook the mixture, covered, for 1 minute. Take the pan from the heat and let the oatmeal stand, covered, until it has thickened—about 1 minute more.

2 Spoon the cereal into 4 individual bowls; add 2 tablespoons of the milk to each bowl and garnish it with the orange segments. Serve the oatmeal at once.

HEALTH NOTE | *This fruity oatmeal is high in soluble fiber, which lowers cholesterol levels.*

SERVES: 4

1⅓ cups fresh orange juice

1 tsp. grated orange zest

1 banana, peeled and coarsely chopped

1⅓ cups quick-cooking rolled oats

½ cup skim milk

1 orange, peeled and segmented

CALORIES: **195**   FAT: **2 G**   SAT. FAT: **.4 G**   CARBOHYDRATES: **39 G**   PROTEIN: **6 G**   CHOLESTEROL: **.6 MG**   SODIUM: **18 MG**   FIBER: **4 G**

SERVES: 4

1 tart apple, cut into small chunks

1 cup plus 1 tbsp. apple cider or
    unsweetened apple juice

1 tbsp. currants or raisins

¼ tsp. ground cinnamon

¼ tsp. salt

1 cup bulgur

Low-fat (1%) milk (optional)

1 Put the apple chunks into a heavy-bottomed saucepan. Add the cider or apple juice, 1 cup of water, currants or raisins, cinnamon, and salt; bring the mixture to a boil. Stir in the bulgur, then cover the pan and reduce the heat to medium-low. Simmer the bulgur mixture until all of the liquid is absorbed—about 15 minutes.

2 Spoon the bulgur into individual serving bowls. If you like, serve the cereal with low-fat milk.

HEALTH NOTE | *Cooked whole grains are an excellent source of fiber and other essential nutrients and are a wonderful breakfast option. This recipe uses bulgur, a form of cracked wheat, but feel free to improvise with other grains, or with bran, which cooks up much faster.*

CALORIES: 178   FAT: .6 G   SAT. FAT: .1 G   CARBOHYDRATES: 41 G   PROTEIN: 4 G   CHOLESTEROL: 0 MG   SODIUM: 151 MG   FIBER: 7 G

CINNAMON

APPLE

CURRANTS

1 Preheat the oven to 400°. Lightly oil 10 muffin-pan cups or 6 mini-Bundt pans.

2 Sift the cake flour, whole-wheat flour, sugar, baking soda, and salt into a bowl; stir in the poppy seeds. In another bowl, combine the ricotta, oil, lemon zest, and lemon juice, and then whisk in the milk. Add the ricotta mixture to the flour mixture and stir them just until they are blended; do not overmix.

3 Beat the egg whites until they form soft peaks. Stir half of the beaten egg whites into the batter, then fold in the remaining egg whites. Spoon the batter into the prepared pan or pans, filling each cup no more than two-thirds full, and bake the muffins until they are lightly browned—about 15 minutes. Serve the muffins or mini-Bundt cakes immediately.

HEALTH NOTE | *Muffins can be a great on-the-go-breakfast or healthy snack. This lemony version is a delicious way to sneak calcium into your day.*

MAKES 10 MUFFINS OR 6 MINI BUNDT CAKES

1½ cups cake flour

½ cup whole-wheat flour

½ cup sugar

1 tsp. baking soda

¼ tsp. salt

¼ cup poppy seeds

1 cup part-skim ricotta cheese

2 tbsp. canola oil

Grated zest of 1 lemon

1 tbsp. fresh lemon juice

¾ cup skim milk

2 egg whites

CALORIES: 217   FAT: 8 G   SAT. FAT: 2 G   CARBOHYDRATES: 30 G   PROTEIN: 7 G   CHOLESTEROL: 8 MG   SODIUM: 236 MG   FIBER: 1 G

SERVES: 12

1 cup all-purpose flour

½ cup whole-wheat flour

1 tsp. baking powder

½ tsp. baking soda

1 tsp. ground cinnamon

½ tsp. ground allspice

1 egg

½ cup packed brown sugar

¼ cup canola oil

½ cup low-fat (1%) milk

1 cup sweet potato (about 6 oz.),
   peeled, grated, and firmly packed

½ cup currants or raisins
   (optional)

1 Preheat the oven to 350°. Lightly oil an 8-by-4-inch loaf pan.

2 Sift the all-purpose flour, whole-wheat flour, baking powder, baking soda, cinnamon, and allspice into a bowl; set the bowl aside. Put the egg and the sugar into a large bowl and beat the mixture until it is light and fluffy. Gradually add the oil and milk; continue beating for 1 minute. Stir in the grated potato and the currants or raisins, if you are using them. Add the sifted flour mixture, ½ cup at a time, mixing the batter after each addition just until the flour is blended. Spoon the batter into the pan.

3 Bake the loaf until it has shrunk from the sides of the pan and a cake tester inserted into the center comes out clean, about 1 hour. Let the bread stand for 10 minutes before turning it out onto a rack. Cool the bread completely before slicing it.

HEALTH NOTE | *Sweet potatoes are an excellent source of the antioxidant beta carotene. This recipe also uses some whole-wheat flour, which increases the fiber content and adds an excellent source of selenium, another important antioxidant.*

CALORIES: 159   FAT: 6 G   SAT. FAT: .6 G   CARBOHYDRATES: 25 G   PROTEIN: 3 G   CHOLESTEROL: 18 MG   SODIUM: 109 MG   FIBER: 1 G

SMALL
PLATES

SERVES: 12

4 ripe avocados

1 tbsp. fresh lime juice

1 tbsp. extra virgin olive oil

1 pickled hot green chili pepper, finely diced

1 clove garlic, crushed

1 scallion, finely chopped

1 tbsp. finely chopped cilantro

¼ tsp. salt

Freshly ground black pepper

1 Cut the avocados in half and remove the pits. Spoon the flesh into a bowl and mash lightly with a fork—the texture should not be too smooth. Stir in the lime juice and oil, then the chili, garlic, scallion, cilantro, salt, and some freshly ground pepper.

2 Cover the mixture and set it aside for at least 3 hours to allow the chili to permeate the dip. Serve at room temperature.

HEALTH NOTE *The fire-hot taste provided by the chili pepper and the tang of fresh lime juice give this dip a lively, satisfying flavor. Avocados get three-fourths of their calories from fat, but it's heart-healthy monounsaturated fat—the same type found in olive oil.*

CALORIES: 119   FAT: 11 G   SAT. FAT: 2 G   CARBOHYDRATES: 5 G   PROTEIN: 1 G   CHOLESTEROL: 0 MG   SODIUM: 73 MG   FIBER: 1 G

SERVES: 8

4 small pita breads, each split horizontally in half, then cut into triangles

4 cloves garlic, peeled

2 cans (19 oz. each) chickpeas, rinsed and drained

¾ cup plain nonfat yogurt

½ tsp. grated lemon zest

2 tbsp. fresh lemon juice

4 tsp. dark Asian sesame oil

1 tbsp. reduced-fat sour cream

½ tsp. salt

½ tsp. ground coriander

¼ tsp. cayenne

⅛ tsp. ground allspice

2 tsp. chopped fresh parsley

1 cucumber, thinly sliced

1 Preheat the oven to 350°. Place the pita triangles on a baking sheet and bake for 5 to 7 minutes, or until lightly browned and crisp. Set aside.

2 Meanwhile, cook the garlic in a small saucepan of boiling water for 3 minutes. Drain well. Transfer the garlic to a food processor. Add the chickpeas, yogurt, lemon zest, lemon juice, sesame oil, sour cream, salt, coriander, cayenne, and allspice; puree until smooth.

3 Spoon the hummus into a small bowl and sprinkle with parsley. Serve with the toasted pita triangles and cucumber slices.

HEALTH NOTE *If sodium is a concern, leave out the salt—with the zesty seasonings used in this recipe you won't miss it.*

CALORIES: 217   FAT: 5 G   SAT. FAT: .6 G   CARBOHYDRATES: 34 G   PROTEIN: 9 G   CHOLESTEROL: 1 MG   SODIUM: 399 MG   FIBER: 4 G

1 Preheat the oven to 400°. Place the bread on a baking sheet and bake for 7 minutes, until lightly golden and crisp. Set aside.

2 Meanwhile, cook the garlic in a small saucepan of boiling water for 2 minutes. Drain and set aside.

3 Preheat the broiler. Place the eggplant halves, cut sides down, on the broiler rack and broil 6 inches from the heat for 15 minutes, or until the skins are charred and the eggplants are tender. Set aside to cool slightly. When cool enough to handle, peel the eggplants, discarding the skin.

4 Transfer the eggplants to a food processor. Add the toasts, garlic, walnuts, lemon juice, oil, salt, and oregano. Puree until smooth. Spoon the dip into a small serving bowl. Stir in the parsley and serve with the vegetable strips.

HEALTH NOTE | *Nuts, particularly the walnuts used here, are rich in an omega-3 fatty acid that may prevent sudden, fatal heart attacks.*

SERVES: 4

4 slices firm-textured white sandwich bread

3 cloves garlic, peeled

2 eggplants (about 1 lb. each), halved lengthwise

2 tbsp. coarsely chopped walnuts

2 tbsp. fresh lemon juice

2 tsp. extra virgin olive oil

¾ tsp. salt

¾ tsp. dried oregano

¼ cup chopped parsley

2 carrots, quartered lengthwise and cut into 2-inch-long strips

1 red bell pepper, seeded, deribbed, and cut into 2-inch-long strips

1 green bell pepper, seeded, deribbed, and cut into 2-inch-long strips

CALORIES: **200** FAT: **6 G** SAT. FAT: **.8 G** CARBOHYDRATES: **34 G** PROTEIN: **6 G** CHOLESTEROL: **.3 MG** SODIUM: **319 MG** FIBER: **6 G**

MARJORAM

GARLIC

ROSEMARY

1 Cook the potato in a small pot of boiling water until tender, about 12 minutes. Add the garlic during the last 3 minutes of cooking. Drain. Transfer to a large bowl and mash until smooth. Add 2 tablespoons of the lemon juice, the mayonnaise, chicken broth, $1/4$ teaspoon of the rosemary, $1/4$ teaspoon of the marjoram, and the salt. Set aside.

2 In a large pot, combine $3^{1}/_{2}$ cups of water, the remaining 2 tablespoons lemon juice, the remaining $1/2$ teaspoon rosemary, and the remaining $1/2$ teaspoon marjoram. Bring to a boil over high heat.

3 Meanwhile, pull off the tough bottom leaves of the artichoke. With kitchen scissors, snip the sharp, pointed ends from the remaining leaves. With a paring knife, trim off the end of the stem. Add the artichokes to the boiling liquid, cover, and cook until the artichokes are tender, about 25 minutes.

4 Stir the parsley into the garlic sauce and serve with the artichokes.

SERVES: 4

1 large Yukon gold potato (6 oz.), peeled and sliced

4 cloves garlic, peeled

$1/4$ cup fresh lemon juice

3 tbsp. reduced-fat mayonnaise

3 tbsp. fat-free, reduced-sodium chicken broth

$3/4$ tsp. dried rosemary

$3/4$ tsp. dried marjoram

$1/2$ tsp. salt

4 large artichokes

3 tbsp. chopped fresh parsley

HEALTH NOTE *Artichokes are a culinary treat rich in vitamin C, folic acid, and fiber. They are usually served with high-fat sauces, however. Here, they are served with a lighter, garlicky sauce that utilizes potassium-rich potato.*

CALORIES: 130   FAT: 3 G   SAT. FAT: .4 G   CARBOHYDRATES: 25 G   PROTEIN: 6 G   CHOLESTEROL: 0 MG   SODIUM: 394 MG   FIBER: 8 G

SERVES: 4

2 tsp. olive oil

1 cup chopped onion

1 clove garlic, minced

3 cups peeled, diced eggplant

2 cups chopped tomatoes

1 cup diced celery

¾ cup fat-free, reduced-sodium chicken broth

2 tbsp. tomato paste

½ tsp. salt

¼ tsp. freshly ground black pepper

1 tbsp. capers, rinsed, drained, and chopped

2 tsp. red wine vinegar

1 Heat the oil in a large nonstick skillet over high heat until hot but not smoking. Add the onion and garlic and cook until the onion is softened, about 5 minutes.

2 Add the eggplant, 1 cup of the tomatoes, the celery, broth, ¾ cup of water, the tomato paste, salt, and pepper. Bring to a boil, reduce the heat to a simmer, and cook until the sauce is thickened and the vegetables are softened, about 15 minutes.

3 Stir in the remaining 1 cup of tomatoes, the capers, and vinegar. Spoon the caponata into a bowl and serve warm, at room temperature, or chilled.

HEALTH NOTE | *A tangy Sicilian side dish traditionally served at room temperature, caponata is high in fiber and antioxidants.*

CALORIES: **88**   FAT: **3 G**   SAT. FAT: **.4 G**   CARBOHYDRATES: **15 G**   PROTEIN: **3 G**   CHOLESTEROL: **0 MG**   SODIUM: **398 MG**   FIBER: **4 G**

1 Preheat the broiler. Combine the whole eggs, egg whites, beans, scallions, salt, and hot pepper sauce in a blender or food processor and process until smooth.

2 Heat the oil in an ovenproof skillet over medium heat until hot but not smoking. Add the zucchini and cook until crisp-tender, about 5 minutes. Add the mint, basil, peas, and vinegar and cook until fragrant, about 1 minute.

3 Reduce the heat to low, add the egg mixture to the skillet, cover, and cook until the frittata is set around the edges but still liquid in the center, 6 to 8 minutes.

4 Place the skillet under the broiler, about 3 inches from the heat, and cook until the frittata is golden brown and set in the center, about 2 to 5 minutes. Sprinkle with Parmesan cheese and broil for 1 minute. Cut into wedges, divide among 4 plates, and serve.

HEALTH NOTE | *Although egg yolks are high in cholesterol, remember that the cholesterol in foods doesn't raise the cholesterol in your blood as dramatically as does saturated fat. Major health agencies agree that eating four eggs a week is fine, and some studies suggest that if you're healthy it's okay to have an egg a day.*

SERVES: 4

2 whole eggs

5 egg whites

1 cup canned Great Northern or cannellini beans, rinsed and drained

2 scallions, cut into 1-inch pieces

¾ tsp. salt

¼ tsp. hot pepper sauce

2 tsp. olive oil

2 zucchini, quartered lengthwise and thinly sliced

2 tbsp. chopped fresh mint

½ tsp. dried basil

1½ cups frozen green peas

1 tbsp. balsamic vinegar

3 tbsp. freshly grated Parmesan cheese

CALORIES: **203**   FAT: **7 G**   SAT. FAT: **2 G**   CARBOHYDRATES: **20 G**   PROTEIN: **17 G**   CHOLESTEROL: **109 MG**   SODIUM: **473 MG**   FIBER: **6 G**

SERVES: 4

4 large (6-inch) or 8 medium
   (3-inch) Portobello mushrooms

Cooking spray, preferably
   garlic-flavored

1 tbsp. extra virgin olive oil

¾ cup diced red bell pepper

⅓ cup minced shallots or onion

3 cloves garlic, minced

1½ cups fat-free, reduced-sodium
   chicken or vegetable broth

½ cup couscous

2 tsp. chopped fresh rosemary,
   or ½ tsp. dried

Salt and pepper to taste

8 oz. fresh baby spinach leaves

¼ cup freshly grated
   Parmesan cheese

1 Preheat the oven to 400°.

2 Clean the mushrooms with a damp paper towel. Cut off the stems and discard. Scrape out and discard the mushroom gills. Place the mushroom caps, rounded side up, on a baking sheet; coat caps with cooking spray. Bake for 5 minutes. Remove from the oven; preheat the broiler.

3 Meanwhile, heat oil in a large deep skillet over medium-high heat. Add the red pepper, shallots, and garlic; sauté for 5 minutes. Add broth; bring to a boil. Stir in couscous, rosemary, salt, and pepper; simmer for 1 minute. Add the spinach; cover and cook until leaves wilt. Stir well, cover, and remove from the heat. Let stand for 5 minutes or until liquid has been absorbed.

4 Turn the mushrooms over and fill with the couscous mixture. Sprinkle the cheese on top. Broil 4 inches from heat until cheese is golden brown.

HEALTH NOTE | *Equally suitable as an appetizer or a light main course, this meaty-tasting mushroom dish is an excellent source of folic acid and fiber. Use whole-wheat couscous to boost the fiber even more.*

CALORIES: **243**   FAT: **7 G**   SAT. FAT: **2 G**   CARBOHYDRATES: **38 G**   PROTEIN: **12 G**   CHOLESTEROL: **5 MG**   SODIUM: **254 MG**   FIBER: **7 G**

COUSCOUS

SPINACH

PORTOBELLO

1 Preheat the oven to 400°.

2 Combine the potato, onion, salt, and egg in a medium bowl. Press the mixture into the bottom and up the sides of a 10-inch deep-dish pie plate coated with cooking spray. Mist the potato mixture with cooking spray. Bake for 40 minutes. Remove from the oven. Reduce the oven temperature to 350°.

3 Heat the oil in a large nonstick skillet over medium-high heat. Add the onion and fennel; cook for 20 minutes or until golden, stirring frequently. Remove from the heat and let cool slightly.

4 Combine the eggs, milk, Parmesan, sour cream, salt, and pepper in a large bowl, whisking until well blended. Stir in the fennel mixture. Pour into the prepared potato crust. Bake for 45 minutes or until set. Let it stand for 10 minutes.

HEALTH NOTE | *The nutritious crust in this pie is made from potato—an excellent source of potassium. Caramelizing the onions adds a subtle sweetness to the licorice-flavored fennel.*

SERVES: 6

CRUST

3 cups peeled, shredded Russet potato (about 2 large or 3 medium potatoes)

1/3 cup chopped onion

1/8 tsp. salt

1 egg, lightly beaten

Cooking spray

FILLING

1 tsp. olive oil

2 cups sliced onions

1 medium fennel bulb, thinly sliced

4 eggs

1/2 cup skim milk

1/2 cup freshly grated Parmesan cheese

2 tbsp. nonfat sour cream

1/4 tsp. salt

1/4 tsp. freshly ground black pepper

CALORIES: 208   FAT: 8 G   SAT. FAT: 3 G   CARBOHYDRATES: 22 G   PROTEIN: 12 G   CHOLESTEROL: 184 MG   SODIUM: 393 MG   FIBER: 2 G

Tomato Bruschetta

SERVES: 4

8 slices Italian bread

2 cloves garlic

2 large vine-ripened
  tomatoes, diced

¼ cup chopped fresh basil

1 tsp. extra virgin olive oil

½ tsp. salt

¼ tsp. freshly ground black pepper

1 In toaster oven or under the broiler, toast the bread on both sides. Cut
   1 clove of garlic in half and rub both sides of the toast with it. Set aside.

2 Cook the remaining garlic clove in a small pot of boiling water for
   2 minutes. Transfer the garlic to a cutting board and mince. Combine
   the tomatoes, basil, oil, salt, pepper, and garlic in a bowl.

3 Arrange the toast on a platter. Dividing evenly, spoon the tomato mixture
   over the toast and serve.

HEALTH NOTE | *An Italian classic, bruschetta is a heart-healthy food lover's
dream—loaded with ripe tomatoes and their ample supply of the antioxidants
vitamin C and lycopene.*

CALORIES: **115**   FAT: **3 G**   SAT. FAT: **.5 G**   CARBOHYDRATES: **20 G**   PROTEIN: **4 G**   CHOLESTEROL: **0 MG**   SODIUM: **319 MG**   FIBER: **3 G**

TOMATOES

OLIVE OIL

BASIL

1 In a large bowl, sprinkle the yeast over the water; let it stand about 5 minutes. Stir in the salt, 1 tablespoon of the oil, the cornmeal, and 1 cup of the all-purpose flour. Beat with a mixer until the dough is stretchy, 3 to 5 minutes. Stir in $1/2$ cup of whole-wheat flour and another $1/2$ cup of the all-purpose flour.

2 Coat a board with the remaining $1/4$ cup of all-purpose flour and scrape the dough onto it. Knead the dough until smooth and elastic, 7 to 10 minutes. Add a little more flour if the dough sticks.

3 Place the dough in a bowl, cover with plastic wrap, and let rise in a warm spot until doubled, about 45 minutes. Punch the dough down in a bowl to expel the air bubbles. Pour the remaining 1 tablespoon of oil into a 10-by-15-inch baking pan. Turn the dough in the oil to coat, then press and pat the dough to evenly fill the pan. Sprinkle with corn kernels and sage; press them firmly into the dough, using your palm. Separate the onion slices into rings and mix with the lemon juice. Scatter the onion rings over the dough and press them down gently with your palm. Cover the pan lightly with plastic wrap, and let the dough rise in a warm place until puffy, about 30 minutes.

4 Preheat the oven to 400°. Bake the focaccia uncovered on the lowest rack until the dough is well browned on the edges and bottom, about 35 minutes. Sprinkle with cheese and bake just until cheese begins to melt, about 2 minutes. Serve hot, warm, or at room temperature, cut into squares.

SERVES: 12

1 package active dry yeast

1 cup warm (100°) water

$1/2$ tsp. salt

2 tbsp. olive oil

$3/4$ cup cornmeal, preferably stone-ground

$1\frac{3}{4}$ cups all-purpose flour

$1/2$ cup whole-wheat flour

1 cup corn kernels, fresh or frozen

2 tbsp. minced fresh sage leaves

1 small red onion, thinly sliced

1 tbsp. fresh lemon juice

$1/2$ cup shredded Monterey Jack cheese

CALORIES: **162**   FAT: **4 G**   SAT. FAT: **1 G**   CARBOHYDRATES: **27 G**   PROTEIN: **6 G**   CHOLESTEROL: **5 MG**   SODIUM: **126 MG**   FIBER: **4 G**

SOUPS

Gazpacho with Roasted Peppers

1 Preheat the broiler. Broil the peppers 2 to 3 inches below the heat source, turning them often, until they are uniformly blistered and blackened, 12 to 15 minutes. Transfer the peppers to a bowl and cover the bowl with plastic wrap. Let the peppers stand for 5 minutes—the trapped steam will loosen their skin.

2 Make a slit in one of the peppers and pour the juices that have collected inside it into the bowl. Peel the pepper from top to bottom. Halve the pepper lengthwise, then remove and discard the stem, seeds, and ribs. Repeat the procedure with the other pepper.

3 Put the peppers and their juices into a food processor or blender along with the tomatoes, celery, cucumber, garlic, chopped watercress, broth, orange juice, lemon juice, oil, salt, and pepper. Process the mixture in short bursts until a coarse puree results. Transfer the gazpacho to a bowl and refrigerate it for at least 1 hour.

HEALTH NOTE | *Spain's legendary chilled tomato soup is loaded with phyto-chemicals that help fight heart disease. It can be prepared as much as 24 hours in advance.*

SERVES: 4

1 large red bell pepper

1 large green bell pepper

2 vine-ripened tomatoes, peeled, seeded, and coarsely chopped

2 stalks celery, thinly sliced

1 cucumber, peeled, halved lengthwise, seeded, and cut into large chunks

2 cloves garlic, chopped

1 cup coarsely chopped fresh watercress

½ cup fat-free, reduced-sodium vegetable broth

¼ cup fresh orange juice

1 tbsp. fresh lemon juice

1 tbsp. extra virgin olive oil

¼ tsp. salt

Freshly ground black pepper

CALORIES: 83   FAT: 4 G   SAT. FAT: .5 G   CARBOHYDRATES: 12 G   PROTEIN: 2 G   CHOLESTEROL: 0 MG   SODIUM: 184 MG   FIBER: 2 G

SERVES: 4

1 leek, trimmed, split, thoroughly washed to remove all grit, and sliced

1 onion, sliced

1 carrot, sliced

1 stalk celery, sliced

12 black peppercorns

½ tsp. dill seeds

2 cups frozen green peas (about 10 oz.)

1 cup fat-free, reduced-sodium chicken broth

2 oz. smoked salmon, cut into small cubes

2 tbsp. light cream

2 tbsp. finely cut fresh dill

1 Pour 4 cups of water into a large pot; add the leek, onion, carrot, celery, peppercorns, and dill seeds. Slowly bring the liquid to a boil, then reduce the heat and simmer the vegetables for 1 hour. Add the peas, return the liquid to a simmer, and cook the vegetables for 3 minutes more.

2 Puree the contents of the pot in a blender or food processor. Rinse the pot and return the puree to it; stir in the chicken broth, the salmon, and the cream. Bring the soup just to a boil; ladle it into individual soup bowls and garnish each portion with the dill. Serve immediately or cover and refrigerate.

TIP | *When you prepare this hearty soup a day in advance and refrigerate, it becomes even more seductively rich and smoky. If it thickens during refrigeration, thin with additional chicken broth before reheating.*

CALORIES: 134   FAT: 3 G   SAT. FAT: 1 G   CARBOHYDRATES: 20 G   PROTEIN: 8 G   CHOLESTEROL: 8 MG   SODIUM: 543 MG   FIBER: 4 G

PUMPKIN

PARMESAN

SAGE

1 Heat oil in a large saucepan over medium heat until hot but not smoking. Add the onion and garlic and cook, stirring frequently, until the onion is softened, about 7 minutes. Add the sweet potato, stirring to coat. Stir in the broth, 1⅓ cups water, the tomato paste, chili powder, sugar, sage, and salt and bring to a boil. Reduce to a simmer, cover, and cook until the sweet potato is tender, about 15 minutes.

2 Meanwhile, preheat the oven to 400°. Sprinkle the Parmesan over the bread, place on a baking sheet, and bake for 7 minutes, or until the cheese is lightly browned. Cut the bread into 1-inch squares and set aside.

3 Stir the milk and pumpkin into the sweet potato mixture and return to a boil. Reduce to a simmer and cook, uncovered, stirring frequently, until the flavors have blended, about 3 minutes. Stir in the vinegar. Transfer the mixture to a blender or food processor and puree until smooth. Return the puree to the pan and cook over low heat until the soup is heated through, about 3 minutes. Ladle the soup into bowls, sprinkle the croutons on top, and serve.

HEALTH NOTE | *The sweet potato and pumpkin in this soup are packed with beta carotene, a bright orange pigment that acts in concert with vitamin C and other phytochemicals to protect your body from molecules that can harm your arteries.*

SERVES: 6

2 tsp. olive oil

1 large onion, sliced

1 clove garlic, sliced

1 sweet potato (about 10 oz.), peeled and thinly sliced

1⅓ cups fat-free, reduced-sodium chicken broth

3 tbsp. tomato paste

1¼ tsp. chili powder

1 tsp. sugar

¾ tsp. dried sage

½ tsp. salt

2 tbsp. freshly grated Parmesan cheese

2 slices firm-textured white bread

2 cups low-fat (1%) milk

2 cups canned solid-pack pumpkin puree

2 tbsp. rice vinegar or cider vinegar

CALORIES: **174**   FAT: **4 G**   SAT. FAT: **1 G**   CARBOHYDRATES: **30 G**   PROTEIN: **7 G**   CHOLESTEROL: **5 MG**   SODIUM: **435 MG**   FIBER: **4 G**

SHIITAKE

SESAME

GINGER

Hot-and-Sour Soup

1 Whisk together the water and cornstarch in a small bowl; set aside.

2 In a soup pot, bring the broth to a boil; add the mushrooms, bamboo shoots, vinegar, soy sauce, ginger, and pepper. Gently stir in the tofu, reduce the heat and simmer for 4 minutes. Add the cornstarch mixture; bring to a boil. Cook for 1 minute, stirring constantly.

3 Remove from heat and gradually stir in scallions, sesame oil, and egg. Serve immediately.

HEALTH NOTE | *Low in calories but rich in flavor, this easy-to-make Asian soup includes tofu, a soy food shown to lower cholesterol and fight heart disease.*

SERVES: 8

¼ cup water

3 tbsp. cornstarch

3 cans (16 oz. each) fat-free, reduced-sodium chicken broth

1⅔ cups sliced shiitake mushroom caps

½ cup canned bamboo shoots, cut into strips

2 tbsp. rice vinegar

1 tbsp. low-sodium soy sauce

1 tsp. grated peeled fresh ginger

¼ tsp. freshly ground black pepper

1 package (about 12 oz.) reduced-fat, extra-firm tofu, drained and julienned

¼ cup sliced scallions

½ tsp. dark Asian sesame oil

1 egg, lightly beaten

CALORIES: 59   FAT: 1 G   SAT. FAT: .2 G   CARBOHYDRATES: 6 G   PROTEIN: 7 G   CHOLESTEROL: 27 MG   SODIUM: 519 MG   FIBER: .6 G

SERVES: 6

1 tbsp. olive oil

1 medium onion, chopped

3 or 4 cloves garlic, minced

2 cups lentils, washed and picked over for stones

1 bay leaf

Salt to taste

Freshly ground black pepper to taste

1 lb. spinach or chard, stemmed and coarsely chopped

¼ cup chopped fresh parsley

Plain nonfat yogurt, for garnish

1 Heat oil over medium-low heat in a heavy-bottomed soup pot. Add the onion and cook, stirring, until the onion is tender, 3 to 5 minutes. Add half of the garlic and stir about 30 seconds, until the garlic smells fragrant. Stir in the lentils, 2 quarts of water, and the bay leaf. Bring to a boil; reduce heat, cover, and simmer 40 minutes or until the lentils are tender. Stir in remaining garlic, and add salt and freshly ground pepper to taste.

2 Discard the bay leaf. Puree a cup of the lentils in a blender or food processor, and stir mixture back into soup. Add the spinach, cover, and simmer 5 to 10 minutes, stirring occasionally. Stir in parsley and serve. Top each bowl with a dollop of yogurt.

HEALTH NOTE *The main ingredients of this soup—lentils and spinach—are both disease-fighting superstars, rich in folic acid and fiber. Garlic, used here to give great flavor, contains a substance that helps lower cholesterol and prevent the kind of blood clots that can trigger heart attacks.*

CALORIES: **263**   FAT: **3 G**   SAT. FAT: **.4 G**   CARBOHYDRATES: **42 G**   PROTEIN: **20 G**   CHOLESTEROL: **0 MG**   SODIUM: **52 MG**   FIBER: **9 G**

1 Bring the broth to a boil in a large heavy-bottomed saucepan. Add the garlic, half the lemon juice, and a generous grinding of pepper; reduce the heat and add the chicken. Poach the chicken at a simmer until the meat feels springy to the touch, about 5 minutes.

2 Use a slotted spoon to remove the chicken from the poaching liquid. When the chicken is cool enough to handle, cut it into small cubes and put the cubes in a bowl. Toss the chicken with the mint and the remaining lemon juice; set it aside to marinate.

3 Add the tomatoes and thyme to the broth and simmer for 10 minutes. Add the eggplant and cook for 5 minutes more. Stir in the chicken and its marinade and simmer the soup for 2 minutes. Sprinkle the feta on top and serve.

HEALTH NOTE | *There's just enough feta cheese here to add a distinctive flavor without tipping the saturated fat scales.*

SERVES: 4

8 cups low-sodium chicken broth

4 cloves garlic, finely chopped

Juice of 1 lemon

Freshly ground black pepper

4 chicken breast halves, skinned and boned (about 1 lb.)

1 tbsp. chopped fresh mint

2½ lb. vine-ripened tomatoes, peeled, seeded, and coarsely chopped, or 28 oz. canned tomatoes, drained and chopped

1 tbsp. fresh thyme, or 1 tsp. dried thyme leaves

¾ lb. eggplant, cut into ½-inch cubes

2 oz. feta cheese, crumbled

CALORIES: 306   FAT: 8 G   SAT. FAT: 4 G   CARBOHYDRATES: 23 G   PROTEIN: 38 G   CHOLESTEROL: 86 MG   SODIUM: 470 MG   FIBER: 5 G

Spiced Sweet Potato, Cauliflower, and Zucchini Soup

1 Bake one of the sweet potatoes in a preheated 375° oven until it is quite soft, about 1 hour. (Alternatively, microwave the sweet potato on high for 7 minutes. Remove it from the oven, wrap it in aluminum foil, and let it stand for 10 minutes.) When the baked sweet potato is cool enough to handle, peel it and set it aside.

2 Meanwhile, peel the remaining sweet potato and cut it crosswise into thin slices. Set the slices aside. Cut the cauliflower core into chunks and set the chunks aside with the leaves.

3 Put the onion slices, cauliflower chunks and leaves (but not the florets), raw sweet-potato slices, garlic, lemon juice, and some pepper in a large, nonreactive pot. Pour in 8 cups of water and bring the liquid to a boil. Reduce the heat and simmer the mixture; skim off any impurities that have collected on the surface. Add the thyme and cloves, and continue to simmer the liquid until it is reduced by half, about 40 minutes.

4 Strain the liquid through a fine sieve into a bowl, pressing on the vegetables to extract all their juices. Return the strained liquid to the pot; discard the solids.

5 Puree the baked sweet potato in a food processor or blender along with ½ cup of the strained liquid. Whisk the puree into the liquid in the pot. Add the onion chunks, cauliflower florets, allspice, salt, and more pepper. Bring the liquid to a simmer over medium heat for 5 minutes. Add the zucchini rounds and cook the soup until the zucchini is tender, 7 to 10 minutes more. Serve the soup either hot or cold.

SERVES: 6

2 large sweet potatoes (about 1 lb.)

1 small cauliflower (about 1¼ lb.), cored and cut into florets, the core and leaves reserved

3 onions, 2 of them thinly sliced, the other cut into small chunks

1 whole garlic bulb, halved horizontally

Juice of 1 lemon

Freshly ground black pepper

1 tbsp. fresh thyme, or 1 tsp. dried thyme leaves

1 tsp. whole cloves

½ tsp. ground allspice

¼ tsp. salt

2 small zucchini, trimmed and cut into ¾-inch-thick rounds

HEALTH NOTE *Many people avoid sweet potatoes thinking they are too caloric. A serving of this flavorful soup contains only about 100 calories.*

CALORIES: **106**   FAT: **.4 G**   SAT. FAT: **.1 G**   CARBOHYDRATES: **24 G**   PROTEIN: **3 G**   CHOLESTEROL: **0 MG**   SODIUM: **111 MG**   FIBER: **3 G**

SERVES: 6

2 cups dried Great Northern beans, picked over

6 cups reduced-sodium chicken broth

1 onion

1 carrot, halved crosswise

1 stalk celery, halved crosswise

1 leek, trimmed, split, and washed thoroughly to remove all grit

1 bay leaf

2 tsp. fresh thyme, or ½ tsp. dried thyme leaves

1 large garlic head, papery outer skin removed

1 tsp. salt

1 tbsp. extra virgin olive oil

3 ripe plum tomatoes, peeled, seeded, and chopped (about 1 cup)

½ cup chopped fresh parsley, preferably Italian, plus extra for garnish

Freshly ground black pepper

1 Rinse the beans and put them in a large heavy-bottomed pot; cover them with 3 inches of water; discard any beans that float to the surface. Cover the pot, leaving the lid ajar, and bring the liquid to a boil over medium-low heat. Boil the beans for 2 minutes, then turn off the heat and soak the beans, covered, for at least 1 hour. Drain the beans in a colander, then return them to the pot.

2 Pour in the broth, then add the onion, carrot, celery, leek, bay leaf, and thyme. Slowly bring the liquid to a boil over medium-low heat. Reduce the heat to maintain a simmer and cover the pot. When the beans have been simmering for 30 minutes, add the garlic head and the salt. Continue cooking the beans, stirring occasionally, until they are tender, 1 to 1½ hours.

3 Near the end of the cooking time, pour the olive oil into a heavy-bottomed skillet over high heat. Add the tomatoes and cook for 3 to 5 minutes, stirring frequently. Stir in the parsley and set aside.

4 Drain the beans in a sieve set over a large bowl to catch the cooking liquid. Discard all the vegetables but the garlic. Return two-thirds of the cooked beans to the pot. When the garlic is cool enough to handle, separate it into its individual cloves and slip off their skins. Puree the garlic and the remaining beans in a food processor along with 1 cup of the reserved cooking liquid.

5 Transfer the garlic-bean puree to the pot with the beans and carefully stir in the remaining cooking liquid. Reheat the soup over low heat, then fold in the tomato mixture. Cook the soup for 1 to 2 minutes more. Season the soup with some pepper, sprinkle with parsley, and serve immediately.

CALORIES: **189**   FAT: **5 G**   SAT. FAT: **1 G**   CARBOHYDRATES: **25 G**   PROTEIN: **12 G**   CHOLESTEROL: **4 MG**   SODIUM: **857 MG**   FIBER: **7 G**

SERVES: 6

12 ¼-inch-thick slices
  French bread, diagonally cut

Olive oil-flavored cooking spray

1 clove garlic, halved

1 tbsp. olive oil

1 cup chopped onion

1 cup chopped carrot

1 cup chopped celery

1 cup diced baking potato

3 cloves garlic, minced

3 cups fat-free, reduced-sodium
  chicken broth

2 cups shredded green cabbage

2 cups shredded kale

½ tsp. dried oregano

1 can (14½ oz.) tomatoes, chopped

1 small zucchini, halved
  lengthwise and thinly sliced

1 small yellow squash, halved
  lengthwise and thinly sliced

1 can (15 oz.) cannellini or
  other white beans, drained

3 tbsp. freshly grated
  Parmesan cheese

1 Preheat the oven to 350°. Place the bread slices in a single layer on a baking sheet coated with cooking spray. Bake for 7 minutes or until bread is toasted. Rub the slices with the garlic halves and set aside.

2 Heat oil in a stockpot over medium-high heat. Add onion, carrot, celery, potato, and garlic; sauté for 5 minutes. Stir in chicken broth, cabbage, kale, oregano, and tomatoes (with liquid); bring to a boil. Reduce heat and simmer, covered, 10 minutes. Stir in zucchini, yellow squash, and beans. Simmer for 15 minutes or until the zucchini and squash are tender.

3 Arrange 2 toast slices in each of 6 individual bowls. Ladle 1½ cups of stew into each bowl and sprinkle each with 1½ teaspoons of cheese.

HEALTH NOTE | *Getting your 3 to 5 servings of vegetables for the day is a breeze with this nutrient-rich Italian stew. Kale stands out as a star, providing high amounts of beta carotene, vitamin C, and folate.*

CALORIES: **233**   FAT: **5 G**   SAT. FAT: **1 G**   CARBOHYDRATES: **37 G**   PROTEIN: **11 G**   CHOLESTEROL: **2 MG**   SODIUM: **649 MG**   FIBER: **7 G**

Pasta Fagioli

1 Heat oil in a large saucepan over medium-low heat. Add ½ cup of water, the onion, carrot, and celery. Cover and cook for 15 minutes or until tender.

2 Add the pasta, parsley, thyme, salt, pepper, beans, broth, and 1½ cups of water. Cook over medium heat for 5 minutes or until heated through. Ladle into bowls. Sprinkle with the tomato and cheese.

HEALTH NOTE | *The fiber-rich combination of pasta and beans is an Italian tradition and an age-old feature of the heart-healthy Mediterranean diet.*

SERVES: 6

1 tbsp. olive oil

1 cup chopped onion

1 cup thinly sliced carrots

1 cup thinly sliced celery

2 cups cooked farfalle (bow-tie pasta)

¼ cup chopped fresh flat-leaf (Italian) parsley

1 tsp. chopped fresh thyme

¼ tsp. salt

⅛ tsp. freshly ground black pepper

1 can (16 oz.) Great Northern beans

1 can (14¼ oz.) fat-free, reduced-sodium beef or chicken broth

6 tbsp. chopped tomato

6 tsp. freshly grated Parmesan cheese

CALORIES: **211**   FAT: **4 G**   SAT. FAT: **1 G**   CARBOHYDRATES: **35 G**   PROTEIN: **10 G**   CHOLESTEROL: **2 MG**   SODIUM: **348 MG**   FIBER: **6 G**

Barley and Mushroom Broth with Smoked Tofu

SERVES: 4

⅓ cup pearl barley, rinsed
    and drained

1 quart fat-free, reduced-sodium
    vegetable broth

1 tbsp. canola oil

1 small onion, finely chopped

2 small carrots, diced

2 stalks celery, diced

¼ lb. mushrooms, wiped
    clean and sliced

1 tsp. cider vinegar

2 tbsp. tomato paste

5 oz. smoked tofu

Freshly ground black pepper

2 tbsp. chopped parsley

2 tbsp. cut chives

1 Place the barley and the vegetable broth in a large saucepan and bring the liquid to a boil. Lower the heat to maintain a simmer, cover the saucepan, and cook for 30 minutes.

2 Meanwhile, heat the oil in a heavy skillet, add the onion, carrot, and celery, and cook over medium heat for about 10 minutes. Add the mushrooms and cook for 2 minutes more.

3 Add the vegetables, vinegar, and tomato paste to the barley and broth and simmer, covered, for 20 minutes. Add the tofu and simmer, covered, for 10 minutes more. Season the broth to taste with the pepper; stir in the parsley and chives. Serve hot.

HEALTH NOTE | *Both barley, high in fiber, and tofu, packed with soy protein, help to lower cholesterol levels.*

CALORIES: **184**   FAT: **6 G**   SAT. FAT: **0 G**   CARBOHYDRATES: **29 G**   PROTEIN: **6 G**   CHOLESTEROL: **0 MG**   SODIUM: **169 MG**   FIBER: **5 G**

MUSHROOMS

TOFU

BARLEY

Southwest Gumbo

SERVES: 8

8 oz. fresh okra

3 tbsp. olive oil

1 large onion, coarsely chopped

1 cup very finely chopped celery

1 large clove garlic, finely chopped

1 large shallot, finely chopped

3 tbsp. masa harina

1 tsp. each: filé powder, salt,
   sugar, freshly ground black
   pepper, and ground cumin

4 cups fish stock

1 green bell pepper

1 red bell pepper

1 lb. tomatillos

⅓ cup chopped fresh parsley

2 tbsp. finely chopped cilantro

Hot pepper sauce to taste

1 lb. halibut steaks (or sea bass),
   skinned

1 lb. orange roughy fillets

1 lb. medium shrimp

1 Trim the okra and cut it into 1-inch lengths. Heat 1 tablespoon of the oil in a large heavy-bottomed, nonreactive pot over medium-high heat. Add the okra and sauté it, turning frequently, until it is evenly browned, about 5 minutes. Remove the okra and set it aside.

2 Reduce the heat to medium and pour the remaining 2 tablespoons of oil into the pot. Add the onion and celery; cook, covered, until the onion is translucent, about 5 minutes. Add the garlic and shallot; cook, stirring constantly, for 2 minutes more. Sprinkle in the masa harina, filé powder, salt, sugar, black pepper, and cumin. Whisk in the stock and bring the liquid to a boil. Seed and coarsely chop the green and red peppers. Husk and core the tomatillos, then cut them into thin wedges. Add the sautéed okra, the green pepper, red pepper, and tomatillos. Partially cover the pot and reduce the heat to maintain a simmer. Cook the gumbo, stirring occasionally, for 8 to 10 minutes.

3 Add the parsley, cilantro, and hot pepper sauce. Cut the halibut and the orange roughy into 1-inch cubes; peel and devein the shrimp if necessary. Gently stir in the halibut, orange roughy, and shrimp. Cover the pot, reduce the heat to low, and cook the gumbo for 5 minutes more. Serve immediately.

HEALTH NOTE | *Okra is a key ingredient in gumbo. When cooked, okra releases a natural thickener that helps bind the flavors together. It's a good source of vitamin C, folic acid, magnesium, potassium, calcium, and fiber.*

CALORIES: **242**   FAT: **8 G**   SAT. FAT: **1 G**   CARBOHYDRATES: **12 G**   PROTEIN: **30 G**   CHOLESTEROL: **96 MG**   SODIUM: **570 MG**   FIBER: **2 G**

SERVES: 6

1 navel orange, sectioned

1 clove garlic, halved

1 head of curly endive, washed
and dried

3 small heads of Belgian endive,
washed, dried, and sliced
crosswise into ½-inch-wide strips

1 small red onion, thinly sliced

1 tbsp. chopped fresh rosemary, or
1 tsp. crumbled dried rosemary

⅛ tsp. salt

2 tbsp. sherry vinegar or red
wine vinegar

1 tbsp. grainy mustard

1½ tbsp. extra virgin olive oil

1 To section the orange, peel it and remove the white pith and membrane.
Working over a bowl to catch the juices, slice down to the core on either
side of a segment and remove it.

2 Rub the inside of a salad bowl with the cut surfaces of the garlic. Put
the curly endive leaves and Belgian endive in the bowl. Add the onion
and rosemary.

3 Whisk together the salt, reserved orange juice, vinegar, and mustard.
Whisking constantly, pour in the oil in a thin, steady stream to create
an emulsified dressing. Pour the dressing over the greens and orange
segments, toss well, and serve at once.

TIP *Try to use fresh rosemary, which will magnify flavor and help keep added
salt to a minimum.*

SERVES: 4

1/2 cup fat-free, reduced-sodium chicken broth

1/3 cup balsamic vinegar

1 tbsp. olive oil

1 tsp. light brown sugar

1 tbsp. chopped fresh oregano, or 3/4 tsp. dried oregano

1/2 tsp. freshly ground black pepper

1 lb. Russet potatoes, scrubbed

2 packages (9 oz. each) frozen artichoke hearts

1 can (19 oz.) red kidney beans, rinsed and drained

2 stalks celery, thinly sliced

1 red bell pepper, seeded, deribbed, and cut into 1/2-inch squares

1 yellow bell pepper, seeded, deribbed, and cut into 1/2-inch squares

4 oz. provolone cheese, cut into 1/2-inch dice (about 1 cup)

1 Combine the broth, vinegar, oil, brown sugar, oregano, and pepper in a large bowl. Set aside.

2 Bring a large pot of water to a boil over medium heat. Add the potatoes and cook until tender, about 25 minutes. When cool enough to handle but still warm, peel and cut into 1/2-inch cubes. Add the potatoes to the broth mixture.

3 Meanwhile, bring a medium saucepan of water to a boil, add the artichokes and cook until tender, about 5 minutes. Drain well and add to the potatoes. Add the beans, celery and red and yellow bell peppers, tossing to combine. Cover and refrigerate for at least 1 hour or up to 8 hours. Add the provolone and toss. Spoon onto 4 plates and serve at room temperature or chilled.

HEALTH NOTE | *Antipasto salads containing meat or cheese can be high in saturated fat and calories. In this delicious, high-fiber version, chicken broth is used to lighten the vinaigrette dressing.*

CALORIES: **386**   FAT: **12 G**   SAT. FAT: **5 G**   CARBOHYDRATES: **52 G**   PROTEIN: **20 G**   CHOLESTEROL: **20 MG**   SODIUM: **577 MG**   FIBER: **16 G**

ARTICHOKE HEARTS

OREGANO

PROVOLONE

WATERCRESS

PEAR

ROQUEFORT

Pear and Roquefort Salad

1 Combine the nectar, lime juice, honey, ginger, salt, and pepper in a large bowl and stir to blend. Add the pears and toss well to coat. Place the watercress on 4 salad plates, fan the pears on top, and spoon any remaining dressing over the salads.

2 Garnish with the currants, Roquefort, and pecans.

SERVES: 4

1 cup canned pear nectar

2 tbsp. fresh lime juice

1 tsp. honey

1 tsp. minced peeled fresh ginger

¼ tsp. salt

¼ tsp. freshly ground black pepper

4 Bartlett pears, cored and thinly sliced lengthwise

8 oz. watercress, washed, dried, and thick stems trimmed, or 1 head of romaine, washed, dried, and shredded

½ cup currants

2 oz. Roquefort cheese, crumbled (about ¼ cup)

2 tbsp. coarsely chopped pecans, toasted

CALORIES:**286**　FAT:**7 G**　SAT. FAT:**3 G**　CARBOHYDRATES:**55 G**　PROTEIN:**6 G**　CHOLESTEROL:**13 MG**　SODIUM:**284 MG**　FIBER:**7 G**

1 Cut the corn kernels from the ears of corn in strips and break into individual kernels. You should have about 4 cups.

2 Combine the vinegar, honey, salt, and jalapeño pepper in a large bowl. Add the corn, tomatoes, celery, bell peppers, onion, parsley, and cheese. Toss to combine and serve.

SERVES: 4

4 ears corn, cooked, or 4 cups no-salt-added canned corn kernels, drained

1/3 cup balsamic vinegar

2 tbsp. honey

1/2 tsp. salt

1 pickled jalapeño chili pepper, finely chopped

2 cups cherry tomatoes, halved

2 stalks celery, thinly sliced

1 red bell pepper, seeded, deribbed, and cut into 1/2-inch squares

1 green bell pepper, seeded, deribbed, and cut into 1/2-inch squares

1 red onion, finely chopped

1/4 cup chopped fresh parsley

3 oz. Monterey Jack cheese, cut into 1/4-inch dice (about 3/4 cup)

SERVES: 12

2½ cups fat-free, low-sodium chicken broth or water

1½ cups long-grain rice

¼ tsp. saffron threads, soaked for 10 minutes in very hot water

1 strip of lemon zest

1 lb. fresh peas, shelled, or 1 cup frozen

¼ cup whole unskinned almonds

1 tsp. Dijon mustard

2 tbsp. red wine vinegar

Freshly ground black pepper

¼ cup olive oil

1 can (15½ oz.) chickpeas, rinsed and well drained

1 red bell pepper, cored and thinly sliced

1 green bell pepper, cored and thinly sliced

2 vine-ripened tomatoes, seeded and chopped

6 oil-cured black olives, thinly sliced

1 Bring the broth to a boil in a medium saucepan over medium heat. Stir in the rice, the saffron and its soaking liquid, and the lemon zest strip. Cover the pan, reduce the heat to medium-low, and simmer until the rice is tender, about 18 minutes. Discard the lemon zest strip. Fluff the rice and set aside to cool.

2 Cook the fresh peas in boiling water until they are just tender, 3 to 5 minutes. Drain and set aside. (If using frozen peas, simply thaw them under running water.)

3 Toast the almonds in a small heavy-bottomed skillet over medium heat until they are fragrant and lightly toasted, about 5 minutes. Remove the almonds from the pan to avoid scorching.

4 In a large mixing bowl, whisk together the mustard, vinegar, and black pepper to taste. Add the oil in a thin, steady stream, whisking vigorously. Add the rice, peas, almonds, chickpeas, red and green peppers, tomatoes, and olives; toss well to coat. Transfer to a serving dish. Serve at room temperature or lightly chilled.

HEALTH NOTE | *This hearty salad is a great source of fiber and antioxidants. The almonds, like most nuts, are packed with beneficial fat and terrific flavor.*

CALORIES: 281   FAT: 18 G   SAT. FAT: 2 G   CARBOHYDRATES: 27 G   PROTEIN: 5 G   CHOLESTEROL: 1 MG   SODIUM: 296 MG   FIBER: 3 G

Red and White Bean Salad

1 Put the kidney beans and the Great Northern beans in a large pot and add just enough water to cover the beans by 3 inches. Bring to a boil for 2 minutes, turn off the heat, and soak the beans, covered, for at least 1 hour. Drain and add enough water to cover the beans by 3 inches. Bring to a boil, reduce the heat, and simmer until they are just tender, 50 to 60 minutes.

2 While the beans are cooking, peel the celery root and cut it into $\frac{1}{2}$-inch cubes. Transfer the cubes to a salad bowl and toss. Add the onion, ginger, and vinegar, Let stand at room temperature.

3 Drain the cooked beans, rinse under cold water, and drain again. Add to the bowl. Add the salt, pepper to taste, the cilantro, tomato, and oil; mix well. Serve chilled or at room temperature.

HEALTH NOTE | *This satisfying salad has plenty of flavor and is also high in soluble fiber.*

SERVES: 8

8 oz. dried red kidney beans, rinsed and drained

8 oz. dried Great Northern beans, rinsed and drained

1 small celery root

1 small onion, thinly sliced

2 tsp. finely chopped peeled fresh ginger

$\frac{1}{4}$ cup red wine vinegar

$\frac{1}{4}$ tsp. salt

Freshly ground black pepper

1 tbsp. chopped fresh cilantro

1 large tomato, chopped

$1\frac{1}{2}$ tbsp. canola oil

CALORIES: 237   FAT: 3 G   SAT. FAT: 0 G   CARBOHYDRATES: 40 G   PROTEIN: 14 G   CHOLESTEROL: 0 MG   SODIUM: 114 MG   FIBER: 15 G

SERVES: 6

2 cups dry whole-wheat pasta

3 tbsp. cider vinegar

2 tbsp. brown sugar

1½ tbsp. olive oil

1 tsp. Dijon mustard

¼ tsp. crushed red pepper

3 cups tightly packed torn fresh
spinach leaves

1 medium pear, cored and sliced
(about 1 cup)

1 small yellow summer squash,
scrubbed and sliced (about 1 cup)

¼ cup sliced red onion

3 tbsp. crumbled feta cheese

1 Cook the pasta as directed on the package and drain. Rinse the pasta under cold water and drain again. Transfer the pasta to a large bowl.

2 Combine the vinegar, brown sugar, olive oil, 1 tablespoon of water, the mustard, and red pepper in a container with a tight-fitting lid. Cover and shake well. Add to the pasta and toss gently. Cover and refrigerate for at least 2 hours or up to 24 hours.

3 Add the spinach, pear, squash, and onion just before serving and toss gently. Divide among 6 salad plates and sprinkle the cheese on each.

HEALTH NOTE | *This eye-pleasing, sweet-and-savory salad is rich in beta carotene, folic acid, and vitamin C.*

CALORIES:**199**   FAT:**5 G**   SAT. FAT:**1 G**   CARBOHYDRATES:**35 G**   PROTEIN:**7 G**   CHOLESTEROL:**4 MG**   SODIUM:**129 MG**   FIBER:**6 G**

PASTA

SQUASH

FETA

Potato, Leek, and Asparagus Salad

SERVES: 4

3 leeks

1½ lb. new potatoes, scrubbed
and cut into 1-inch chunks

¾ tsp. salt

1¼ lb. asparagus, trimmed
and cut on the diagonal into
1-inch lengths

⅔ cup reduced-sodium
vegetable broth

2 tbsp. red wine vinegar

1 tbsp. Dijon mustard

1 tbsp. extra virgin olive oil

¼ cup chopped fresh dill

8 oz. mushrooms, thinly sliced

½ cup crumbled feta cheese (2 oz.)

1 Trim away the roots and dark green leaves of the leeks and cut them lengthwise in half. Cut crosswise into 1-inch pieces. Place in a bowl of lukewarm water and let stand for 1 to 2 minutes. Lift the leeks out of the water, leaving the dirt behind. Repeat if necessary. Set aside.

2 Put the potatoes in a large pot, add ¼ teaspoon of the salt and water to cover. Bring to a boil over medium heat, reduce the heat, cover, and simmer until tender, about 10 minutes. Add the asparagus and leeks during the last 2 minutes of cooking time. Drain well.

3 Combine the broth, vinegar, mustard, oil, and the remaining ½ teaspoon salt in a large bowl. Stir in the dill. Add the potatoes, asparagus, leeks, and mushrooms, tossing gently to coat. Spoon onto 4 plates, sprinkle with the feta, and serve at room temperature.

TIP *If you can't find leeks, you can make this salad with 12 scallions, blanched for 30 seconds and cut into 1-inch lengths. Leeks and other onion-family vegetables are rich in anticlotting compounds that help prevent heart attacks.*

Lentil Salad with **Red Bell Peppers**

SERVES: 12

1½ cups dried lentils, picked over and rinsed

¼ cup finely chopped fresh tarragon, or 2 tbsp. dried tarragon

¼ cup tarragon vinegar

3 red bell peppers

¼ cup extra virgin olive oil

8 large cloves garlic, unpeeled

¾ cup fresh lemon juice

¼ cup finely sliced fresh chives or scallions

3 tbsp. very finely chopped fresh chervil (optional)

¾ tsp. salt

Freshly ground black pepper

1 hard-cooked egg

1 cucumber, preferably unwaxed

3 small ripe tomatoes, sliced

HEALTH NOTE | *Lentils cook faster than any of their bean-family kin and offer lots of cholesterol-lowering fiber and folic acid.*

1 Put the lentils in a large heavy-bottomed pot with 3 cups of water. Bring to a boil over high heat, reduce the heat, and simmer until tender, about 20 minutes. If using dried tarragon, combine it with the vinegar in a small nonreactive pan. Bring the liquid to a simmer over medium heat, remove the pan from the heat, and steep the tarragon for at least 10 minutes.

2 Preheat the broiler. Roast the peppers about 2 inches below the heat, turning until blistered on all sides. Place the peppers in a bowl and cover with plastic wrap; the trapped steam will loosen their skins. Peel, seed, and finely chop the peppers; set aside. Drain the lentils and transfer them to a large bowl. Combine the oil and vinegar in a small bowl and pour the liquid over the lentils. Add the chopped peppers and stir the mixture well, then refrigerate it.

3 Preheat the oven to 500°. Bake the garlic cloves in a small, ovenproof dish until soft, 7 to 10 minutes. When they are cool enough to handle, peel and press them through a sieve into a bowl. Whisk the lemon juice into the garlic puree and stir the puree into the lentil-pepper mixture. Add the chives or scallions, fresh tarragon, salt, some pepper, and chervil, if desired; stir the mixture well. Refrigerate for at least 2 hours.

4 To serve, peel the egg and separate the yolk from the white. Press the yolk through a sieve into a small bowl. Sieve the egg white the same way. Mound the salad on a serving plate; sprinkle half of the egg white and then half of the yolk over the top. With a vegetable peeler, pare strips of the cucumber skin to achieve a striped effect. Garnish the salad with thinly sliced cucumber and tomatoes.

CALORIES: **151**   FAT: **6 G**   SAT. FAT: **.8 G**   CARBOHYDRATES: **19 G**   PROTEIN: **8 G**   CHOLESTEROL: **18 MG**   SODIUM: **157 MG**   FIBER: **4 G**

Broiled Tuna and Pepper Salad

1 Preheat the broiler.

2 Brush the tuna with the broth and broil it 6 inches from the heat, turning once, until just barely opaque, about 5 minutes. Let cool, then cut into bite-size pieces.

3 Bring a small pot of water to a boil, add the garlic, and cook for 2 minutes. Drain and finely chop. Combine the garlic, tomato-vegetable juice, vinegar, oil, basil, and pepper in a large bowl. Stir in the beans, red and yellow bell peppers, tomatoes, radishes, and scallions, tossing to coat thoroughly. Gently fold in the tuna and serve warm, at room temperature, or chilled.

HEALTH NOTE | *This enticing salad helps fight heart disease with antioxidant-rich bell pepper and fiber-packed beans. Some types of tuna are better sources of healthful omega-3 fats than others; albacore is one of the best.*

SERVES: 4

¾ lb. tuna steak

¼ cup fat-free, reduced-sodium chicken broth

2 cloves garlic

½ cup low-sodium tomato-vegetable juice

2 tbsp. wine vinegar

1 tbsp. olive oil

3 tbsp. chopped fresh basil

½ tsp. freshly ground black pepper

1 can (19 oz.) white beans (cannellini), rinsed and drained

1 red bell pepper, seeded, deribbed, and diced

1 yellow bell pepper, seeded, deribbed, and diced

2 tomatoes, seeded and diced

1 cup sliced radishes

½ cup sliced scallions

CALORIES: **292**   FAT: **9 G**   SAT. FAT: **2 G**   CARBOHYDRATES: **25 G**   PROTEIN: **29 G**   CHOLESTEROL: **32 MG**   SODIUM: **277 MG**   FIBER: **8 G**

MANGO

PINEAPPLE

SHRIMP

1 Peel the mangoes and slice the flesh into large cubes. Puree one-quarter of the flesh in a food processor or blender, then pass it through a sieve set over a bowl. Refrigerate the puree. Add the remaining mango pieces, the pineapple, lime juice, and chopped cilantro; stir, cover, and refrigerate the mango-pineapple relish.

2 Bring 2 quarts of water to a boil in a large saucepan. Add the shrimp and cook until opaque, about 1 minute. Drain and refresh under cold water. Transfer the shrimp to a bowl. Add the peppers to the shrimp. Stir the mango puree, mayonnaise, scallions, ginger, and salt into the shrimp mixture. Refrigerate for at least 30 minutes.

3 To serve, spoon some of the relish onto a large platter and surround it with some of the shrimp salad. Top the relish with the remaining shrimp salad.

HEALTH NOTE | *You may think shrimp is a no-no. While it does contain more cholesterol than other fish and meat, it is extremely low in cholesterol-raising saturated fat and overall fat—so enjoy!*

SERVES: 8

2 large ripe mangoes

1 pineapple, peeled and cut into ¼-inch cubes

¼ cup fresh lime juice

½ cup finely chopped fresh cilantro

1½ lb. medium shrimp, peeled and deveined if necessary

2 red bell peppers, seeded, deribbed, and diced

¼ cup reduced-fat mayonnaise

4 scallions, thinly sliced

2 tbsp. grated peeled fresh ginger

½ tsp. salt

CALORIES: **211**   FAT: **3 G**   SAT. FAT: **.5 G**   CARBOHYDRATES: **32 G**   PROTEIN: **15 G**   CHOLESTEROL: **105 MG**   SODIUM: **312 MG**   FIBER: **3 G**

1 Combine the orange juice, olive oil, honey, salt, and peppercorns in a large bowl and whisk well. Add the shrimp. Cover and marinate, refrigerated, for 1 hour.

2 Combine 4 cups of water and the bulgur in a large bowl. Cover and let stand for 30 minutes.

3 Drain well. Add to the shrimp. Add the spinach, cucumber, orange segments, onion, mint, and parsley. Cover and marinate, refrigerated, for at least 1 hour, stirring occasionally.

HEALTH NOTE | *There is evidence that whole grains like bulgur help prevent heart disease. This vitamin C-rich salad also provides a good dose of folic acid, vitamin E, and fiber.*

SERVES: 8

$2/3$ cup fresh orange juice
(about 2 oranges)

2 tbsp. olive oil

1 tbsp. honey

$1/2$ tsp. salt

$1/4$ tsp. cracked black peppercorns

1 lb. peeled cooked shrimp

1 cup bulgur

2 cups thinly sliced spinach

1 cup diced, seeded, and peeled cucumber

3 navel oranges, sectioned

$1/2$ cup thinly sliced red onion

$2/3$ cup chopped fresh mint

$1/3$ cup chopped fresh parsley

CALORIES: **188**   FAT: **4 G**   SAT. FAT: **.7 G**   CARBOHYDRATES: **23 G**   PROTEIN: **15 G**   CHOLESTEROL: **111 MG**   SODIUM: **292 MG**   FIBER: **5 G**

Margarita Scallop Salad

SERVES: 4

3 tbsp. fresh lime juice

2 tbsp. minced fresh parsley

1 tsp. dried basil

1 lb. sea scallops

¼ cup fat-free, reduced-sodium chicken broth

2 tbsp. olive oil

¼ cup fresh orange juice

1 tbsp. tequila

¼ tsp. salt

¼ tsp. freshly ground black pepper

1½ cups cherry tomatoes, halved

½ sweet onion, halved and thinly sliced

1 cup thinly sliced cucumber

1½ cups frozen corn kernels, thawed

Cooking oil spray

2 cups mixed baby salad greens or mixed torn greens

1 Combine 2 tablespoons of the lime juice, the parsley, and basil in a medium bowl. Add the scallops, tossing to coat. Let stand at room temperature for 10 minutes.

2 Combine the broth, oil, orange juice, tequila, salt, pepper, and the remaining 1 tablespoon lime juice in a large bowl. Add the tomatoes, onion, cucumber, and corn, tossing to coat.

3 Preheat the grill. Spray the rack, off the grill, with cooking oil spray.

4 Thread the scallops onto 8 skewers. Place the skewers on the rack and grill until the scallops are just opaque, 2 to 3 minutes. Turn and grill the second side until opaque, 2 to 3 minutes. Spread the salad greens on a platter and top with the tomato mixture and the scallops and serve warm or at room temperature.

HEALTH NOTE | *Scallops have no saturated fat and very little total fat. All the fat in this salad comes from heart-healthy, monounsaturated olive oil.*

CALORIES: 267   FAT: 8 G   SAT. FAT: 1 G   CARBOHYDRATES: 25 G   PROTEIN: 23 G   CHOLESTEROL: 37 MG   SODIUM: 379 MG   FIBER: 3 G

SERVES: 6

1 tbsp. olive oil

1 medium sweet onion

$\frac{1}{2}$ to 1 tsp. salt

2$\frac{1}{2}$ cups diced yellow zucchini

2$\frac{1}{2}$ cups diced green zucchini

3 large cloves garlic, minced

1 Anaheim chili pepper, seeded and finely chopped

1 jalapeño chili pepper, seeded and finely chopped

6 medium tomatoes, peeled, seeded, and chopped

2 cups fresh or frozen corn kernels, preferably white (2 ears of corn)

$\frac{1}{2}$ cup chopped fresh cilantro

1 cup canned pinto or black beans, rinsed and drained

12 corn tortillas

$\frac{1}{2}$ cup nonfat cottage cheese

2 tbsp. yogurt

1 Heat the oil in a large nonstick skillet over medium heat. Add the onion and cook, stirring, until translucent, about 5 minutes. Add $\frac{1}{2}$ teaspoon of the salt and the yellow and green zucchini, stir together, and cook until the zucchini begins to soften. Add a few tablespoons of water if the vegetables stick to the pan. Add the garlic and stir until it begins to smell fragrant, about 1 minute. Add the chilies and two-thirds of the tomatoes, reduce the heat to medium-low and cook, stirring often, until the vegetables are tender. Add the corn and cook until crisp-tender, about 3 minutes. Add all but 2 tablespoons of the cilantro, the remaining tomatoes, and the beans. Stir, taste, and adjust the salt; remove from heat.

2 Wrap the tortillas in plastic wrap and heat in the microwave until warm, about 45 seconds. Blend the cottage cheese with the yogurt. Spread the vegetables on the tortillas, top each with 1 tablespoon of the cottage-cheese mixture, garnish with the remaining cilantro, and serve.

TIP *Always handle jalapeños and other hot peppers with care—making sure to keep the volatile oils that give this tasty chili its zing away from your face, lips, and eyes.*

CALORIES: **290**   FAT: **5 G**   SAT. FAT: **.6 G**   CARBOHYDRATES: **54 G**   PROTEIN: **12 G**   CHOLESTEROL: **2 MG**   SODIUM: **464 MG**   FIBER: **9 G**

SERVES: 6

2 tbsp. low-sodium soy sauce

2 tsp. rice vinegar or wine vinegar

1½ tsp. sugar

½ cup reduced-sodium vegetable
broth or water

1½ tsp. cornstarch

½ tsp. hot pepper sauce

2 tbsp. canola oil

2 lb. firm tofu, well drained
and cut into ¾-inch cubes

2 cloves garlic, thinly sliced

1½-inch piece fresh ginger,
peeled and finely grated

3 fresh or dried red chili peppers,
seeded and thinly sliced

8 scallions, thinly sliced, white
and green parts separated

2 small green bell peppers, seeded,
deribbed, and cut into ¾-inch
squares

⅛ tsp. salt

1 tbsp. rice wine or sherry

¼ cup peanuts, toasted

1 In a small bowl, mix the soy sauce, vinegar, sugar, broth, cornstarch, and hot pepper sauce; set this seasoning sauce aside.

2 Heat 2 teaspoons of the oil in a heavy nonstick skillet over medium-high heat. Add half of the tofu cubes and cook, turning constantly to prevent sticking, until golden brown all over, 3 to 5 minutes. Transfer to paper towels and drain. Pour another 2 teaspoons of the oil into the skillet and cook the remaining tofu cubes the same way and drain.

3 Heat the remaining 4 teaspoons of oil in a wok or large heavy-bottomed skillet, swirling it around to coat the sides. Drop in the garlic and allow it to sizzle for a few seconds. Add the ginger and sauté it, stirring constantly, until golden brown, about 2 minutes. Add the chili peppers and the white parts of the scallions and stir-fry for 10 seconds, turning and tossing the ingredients with a spatula. Add the bell peppers and stir-fry for another 10 seconds. Add the tofu cubes and continue to stir-fry for about 20 seconds. Add the salt and the rice wine.

4 Stir the seasoning sauce well and pour it into the wok. Continue to stir until the sauce thickens. Add the peanuts and mix them in. Remove the wok from the heat and mix in most of the green parts of the scallions. Transfer the stir-fry to a serving dish, and sprinkle with the remaining scallions.

HEALTH NOTE | *Most nuts are sources of good fat and good flavor. This includes peanuts, which are technically legumes.*

CALORIES: 339   FAT: 21 G   SAT. FAT: 3 G   CARBOHYDRATES: 16 G   PROTEIN: 27 G   CHOLESTEROL: 0 MG   SODIUM: 294 MG   FIBER: 5 G

GINGER

PEANUTS

SCALLIONS

Mediterranean Gyros

1 Put the chickpeas in the bowl of a food processor, add 3 tablespoons water, the lemon juice and garlic, and process until smooth, scraping down the sides of the bowl. Set aside.

2 Heat the oil in a large nonstick skillet over medium-high heat. Add the onion, red and green pepper strips, and mushrooms; sauté until the vegetables are tender, about 6 minutes.

3 Wrap the pita breads in plastic wrap and microwave on high until heated, about 45 seconds.

4 Spread about 2 tablespoons of the bean mixture over each pita bread. Top each with 1/2 cup of the onion mixture, 2 tablespoons tomato, 1 tablespoon cheese, and 1 1/2 teaspoons chopped olives. Fold in half, secure with a toothpick, and serve.

HEALTH NOTE | *Chickpeas are used to replace the saturated fat-laden meat typically found in restaurant gyros. This gyro is also veggie-packed, providing lots of vitamins and fiber.*

SERVES: 8

1 can (15 oz.) chickpeas, rinsed and drained

2 tbsp. fresh lemon juice

2 cloves garlic

1 tsp. olive oil

1 1/2 cups thinly sliced onion

1 1/2 cups red bell pepper strips

1 1/2 cups green bell pepper strips

1 cup sliced mushrooms

8 pita breads (8 inches each)

1 cup chopped tomato

2 oz. feta cheese with basil and tomato, crumbled

1/4 cup chopped black olives

CALORIES: **260**   FAT: **4 G**   SAT. FAT: **1 G**   CARBOHYDRATES: **46 G**   PROTEIN: **9 G**   CHOLESTEROL: **6 MG**   SODIUM: **501 MG**   FIBER: **4 G**

SERVES: 4

2 ripe mangoes, peeled, pitted, and coarsely chopped

1 small red bell pepper, seeded, deribbed, and coarsely chopped

1 small red onion, minced

¼ cup chopped fresh cilantro

1 medium clove garlic, minced

¼ cup pineapple juice

6 tbsp. fresh lime juice

Salt

1 or 2 jalapeño peppers, finely chopped

4 salmon fillets (6 oz. each)

Olive or canola oil

2 tbsp. ground cumin

Freshly ground black pepper

Sprigs of cilantro, for garnish

1 Combine the mangoes, bell pepper, onion, cilantro, garlic, pineapple juice, and lime juice in a medium bowl. Mix well and season to taste with salt and jalapeño. Set aside the salsa.

2 Prepare the grill and heat to medium-hot.

3 Coat the salmon fillets lightly with oil, rub with cumin, and sprinkle with salt and pepper to taste. Place the fish on the grill and cook for 6 to 8 minutes per side. To check doneness, cut into 1 fillet; it should be opaque throughout.

4 Remove the salmon from the grill and top each fillet generously with salsa. Garnish with several cilantro sprigs and serve, passing the remaining salsa separately.

HEALTH NOTE | *Salmon is a rich source of disease-fighting fish oils called omega-3 fats. They help prevent heart attacks by lessening the tendency of your blood to form dangerous clots.*

CALORIES: **483**   FAT: **26 G**   SAT. FAT: **5 G**   CARBOHYDRATES: **27 G**   PROTEIN: **36 G**   CHOLESTEROL: **100 MG**   SODIUM: **112 MG**   FIBER: **2 G**

SCALLOPS

LINGUINE

MINT

1 Toss the carrots with the orange juice concentrate and refrigerate in a covered container for up to 8 hours.

2 Bring a large pot of water to a boil over medium-high heat, add the linguine, and cook as directed on the package, until al dente. Drain.

3 Meanwhile, heat the oil in a large nonstick skillet over medium heat until hot but not smoking. Add the scallops and garlic and cook, stirring, until the scallops are just opaque, about 3 minutes. Using a slotted spoon, transfer the scallops to a plate. Add the tomatoes, clam juice, salt, and pepper to the skillet. Bring to a boil, stir in the carrots, reduce the heat, and simmer, stirring from time to time, until the sauce is thickened and slightly reduced, about 5 minutes. Return the scallops to the skillet. Add the mint and cook until the scallops are warmed through, about 1 minute. Transfer the sauce to a large bowl, add the pasta, and toss. Divide among 4 bowls and serve.

SERVES: 4

8 oz. carrots, shredded (about 1 cup)

1 tbsp. frozen orange juice concentrate

8 oz. dry linguine

2 tsp. olive oil

12 oz. bay scallops or quartered sea scallops

1 clove garlic, minced

1 can (14½ oz.) no-salt-added stewed tomatoes

½ cup bottled clam juice

¼ tsp. salt

¼ tsp. freshly ground black pepper

2 tbsp. chopped fresh mint

CALORIES:354   FAT:4 G   SAT. FAT:.5 G   CARBOHYDRATES:56 G   PROTEIN:23 G   CHOLESTEROL:28 MG   SODIUM:377 MG   FIBER:5 G

Salmon Steaks with Pesto and Peppers

SERVES: 4

1 cup fat-free, reduced-sodium
  chicken broth

5 cloves garlic

1 tbsp. olive oil

2 cups (packed) fresh basil leaves

2 tbsp. grated Parmesan cheese

2 tbsp. plain dried breadcrumbs

1 tbsp. fresh lemon juice

$\frac{1}{2}$ tsp. salt

$\frac{1}{4}$ tsp. freshly ground black pepper

2 cups frozen corn kernels, thawed

4 scallions, sliced

Cooking oil spray

4 bell peppers, mixed colors, halved
  lengthwise, stems left on, seeded,
  and deribbed

4 salmon steaks (1 lb. total)

1 lemon, cut into wedges,
  for garnish

1 Combine the broth, garlic, and olive oil in a medium saucepan and bring to a boil over medium-high heat. Cook until reduced to $\frac{1}{4}$ cup, 12 to 15 minutes. Let cool slightly and pour into a blender or food processor. Add the basil, Parmesan, breadcrumbs, lemon juice, salt, and pepper and process until smooth. Place the corn, scallions, and half of the pesto in a medium bowl and toss to combine.

2 Preheat the grill to medium. Spray the rack, off the grill, with cooking oil spray.

3 Grill the pepper halves, cut side down, for 8 minutes. Invert them and spoon the corn mixture into them, dividing evenly. You may want to do this off the grill. Place the peppers toward the outer edges of the grill to cook while you grill the salmon.

4 Brush the salmon steaks lightly with some of the remaining pesto. Grill the salmon, turning once and basting liberally with the remaining pesto, until just opaque, about 12 minutes. Place the salmon and peppers on 4 plates and serve with lemon wedges.

HEALTH NOTE | *Salmon is a particularly good source of beneficial omega-3 fats. Pesto, a versatile sauce whose key ingredient is olive oil, can be very high in calories. This slimmed-down version uses chicken broth to reduce the amount of oil.*

CALORIES: 398   FAT: 18 G   SAT. FAT: 4 G   CARBOHYDRATES: 34 G   PROTEIN: 31 G   CHOLESTEROL: 69 MG   SODIUM: 452 MG   FIBER: 7 G

SERVES: 4

½ tsp. saffron threads

2 tsp. olive oil

1 cup diced onion

4 cloves garlic, crushed

2 plum tomatoes, peeled, seeded,
   and diced

1 bottle (8 oz.) clam juice

Pinch of crushed red pepper

Pinch of freshly ground
   black pepper

¼ cup raw Arborio or other
   medium-grain rice

2 cups canned artichoke hearts,
   drained and quartered

⅓ cup dry vermouth

16 small mussels, scrubbed

8 medium shrimp, peeled and
   deveined (about 8 oz.)

¼ cup minced fresh
   flat-leaf parsley

1 Soak the saffron for 10 minutes in ¼ cup very hot water.

2 Heat the oil in a large flameproof casserole over medium-high heat. Add the onion and garlic and sauté for 2 minutes. Add the saffron and its liquid, 1 cup of water, the tomatoes, clam juice, red pepper, and black pepper; bring to a boil. Stir in the rice. Cover, reduce the heat, and simmer for 10 minutes.

3 Add the artichokes, vermouth, mussels, and shrimp. Cover and simmer until the mussel shells open, about 5 minutes. Discard any unopened shells. Sprinkle with parsley and serve.

NOTE | *Saffron, the dried stigma of the purple-flowered crocus, is an expensive spice that lends its wonderful, dusky flavor to this paella.*

CALORIES:**297**   FAT:**4 G**   SAT. FAT:**.6 G**   CARBOHYDRATES:**42 G**   PROTEIN:**19 G**   CHOLESTEROL:**77 MG**   SODIUM:**273 MG**   FIBER:**5 G**

SAFFRON

SHRIMP

DRY VERMOUTH

SERVES: 6

1 tbsp. olive oil

3 onions, thinly sliced

5 new potatoes, peeled and
thinly sliced

2 cups fresh or frozen corn kernels

½ green bell pepper, seeded,
deribbed, and diced

Hot pepper sauce

1 lb. cod or haddock or pollock,
skinned, rinsed under cold water,
and cut into chunks

2½ lb. ripe tomatoes, peeled,
seeded, and chopped, or 1 can
(28 oz.) no-salt-added whole
tomatoes, drained and chopped

Salt and freshly ground black pepper

1 Heat the oil in a large heavy-bottomed pot over medium heat. Add a
layer of onions and a layer of potatoes. Sprinkle some of the corn and bell
pepper on top. Dribble a few drops of hot pepper sauce over the vegetables.
Add a layer of fish and a layer of tomatoes and season with salt and pepper.
Repeat until all the vegetables and fish are used.

2 Cover, reduce the heat to medium-low, and cook until the potatoes are
done, about 45 minutes. Serve at once.

CALORIES: **282** FAT: **4 G** SAT. FAT: **.6 G** CARBOHYDRATES: **45 G** PROTEIN: **20 G** CHOLESTEROL: **33 MG** SODIUM: **169 MG** FIBER: **7 G**

Chicken and White Bean Cassoulet

1 Preheat the oven to 375°. Coat a 3-quart casserole with cooking spray.

2 Sprinkle salt and pepper over the chicken. Heat the oil in a large nonstick skillet over medium-high heat. Add the chicken and cook for 2 minutes on each side, or until browned. Cut the chicken into $3/4$-inch cubes and set aside. Cook the bacon in the same skillet over medium-high heat until crisp. Remove from the skillet, crumble, and set aside. Add the cabbage, onions, and garlic to the skillet and sauté until the cabbage is crisp-tender, about 4 minutes.

3 Combine the chicken, cabbage mixture, rosemary, and beans in the casserole and top with the breadcrumbs. Bake until heated through, about 30 minutes. Top with the crumbled bacon and serve.

HEALTH NOTE | *In its classic form, cassoulet, the French bean casserole, cooks for hours in a slow oven and is laden with artery-clogging fat. This quick, light adaptation is every bit as tasty.*

SERVES: 6

Olive oil-flavored cooking spray

$1/4$ tsp. salt

$1/4$ tsp. freshly ground black pepper

12 oz. skinless and boneless chicken breast

1 tbsp. olive oil

2 slices of bacon

6 cups sliced cabbage

3 cups vertically sliced onions

3 cloves garlic, minced

$1/2$ tsp. dried rosemary

1 can (19 oz.) white beans (cannellini), rinsed and drained

$1/2$ cup plain dried breadcrumbs

CALORIES: **304**   FAT: **8 G**   SAT. FAT: **2 G**   CARBOHYDRATES: **35 G**   PROTEIN: **23 G**   CHOLESTEROL: **38 MG**   SODIUM: **255 MG**   FIBER: **3 G**

SERVES: 4

2 tbsp. flour

½ tsp. salt

¼ tsp. freshly ground black pepper

2 bone-in chicken breasts, skinned, halved, and cut in half crosswise (about 1½ lb.)

1 tbsp. extra virgin olive oil

8 oz. orzo

1 large onion, cut into 1-inch chunks

1 Granny Smith apple, halved, cored, and cut into 1-inch chunks

1 tomato, coarsely chopped

½ cup fat-free, reduced-sodium chicken broth

¼ cup chopped fresh mint

1 tbsp. red wine vinegar

½ tsp. ground cinnamon

1 Combine the flour, ¼ teaspoon of the salt, and the pepper on a sheet of wax paper. Dredge the chicken pieces in the flour mixture, shaking off the excess. Heat the oil in a nonstick, nonreactive, ovenproof casserole over medium heat until hot but not smoking. Add the chicken and cook until golden brown, about 4 minutes per side. Using a slotted spoon, transfer the chicken to a plate. Set aside.

2 Bring a large pot of water to a boil, add the orzo, and cook until tender. Drain well.

3 Meanwhile, add the onion to the casserole and cook, stirring frequently, until lightly golden, about 5 minutes. Add the apple and cook, stirring frequently, until slightly softened, about 4 minutes. Stir in the tomato, broth, mint, vinegar, cinnamon, and the remaining ¼ teaspoon salt. Bring to a boil, return the chicken to the casserole, and reduce to a simmer. Cover and cook until the chicken is cooked through, about 8 minutes. Divide the orzo among 4 bowls, spoon the chicken mixture on top or alongside, and serve.

HEALTH NOTE | *Chicken is very low in saturated fat compared with other meats; the breast is the leanest part. Here it is prepared with a tasty sauce and served with orzo, a small pasta in the shape of rice grains.*

CALORIES: 452   FAT: 6 G   SAT. FAT: 1 G   CARBOHYDRATES: 58 G   PROTEIN: 39 G   CHOLESTEROL: 76 MG   SODIUM: 462 MG   FIBER: 4 G

ROSEMARY

BASIL

CANNELLINI

Panzanella with Grilled Chicken

1 Combine the oil, vinegar, rosemary, garlic, salt, and pepper in a bowl and mix well with a fork or shake in a jar with a tight-fitting lid. Place the chicken on a plate and brush 1 tablespoon of the oil mixture over it, turning to coat. Cover and refrigerate the chicken and the remaining oil mixture for at least 10 minutes or up to 8 hours.

2 Preheat the grill to medium.

3 Place the chicken on the grill and pour any remaining marinade from the plate over the chicken. Grill, turning once, until the chicken is no longer pink in the center, about 5 minutes on each side. Using 1 tablespoon of the oil mixture, brush both sides of the bread and grill, turning once, until lightly toasted.

4 Combine the beans, lettuce, tomato, and basil in a large bowl. Add the remaining oil mixture and toss well. Cut the toast into cubes, add to the salad, and toss again. Divide among 4 serving plates and top with the chicken. Season with more pepper if desired and serve.

NOTE | *This flavorful chicken is served on top of a salad. Marinating the meat before grilling maximizes flavor.*

SERVES: 4

3 tbsp. extra virgin olive oil

3 tbsp. balsamic vinegar

1 tsp. dried rosemary, crushed

1 clove garlic, minced

$\frac{1}{2}$ tsp. salt

$\frac{1}{2}$ tsp. freshly ground black pepper

4 skinless and boneless chicken breast halves

2 large slices of Italian bread, or 4 slices of French baguette

1 cup white beans (cannellini)

4 cups torn romaine lettuce

2 cups chopped tomato

$\frac{1}{3}$ cup chopped fresh basil

CALORIES: 374   FAT: 14 G   SAT. FAT: 2 G   CARBOHYDRATES: 29 G   PROTEIN: 34 G   CHOLESTEROL: 66 MG   SODIUM: 483 MG   FIBER: 6 G

SERVES: 4

3 oz. (1 link) Italian turkey
  sausage, casing removed

2/3 cup yellow cornmeal

1/4 tsp. freshly ground black pepper

1 can (10 1/2 oz.) fat-free,
  reduced-sodium chicken broth

2 tbsp. chopped fresh
  flat-leaf parsley

Cooking spray

1 tbsp. balsamic vinegar

1 tbsp. olive oil

1/4 tsp. salt

8 oz. mushrooms, sliced
  (about 3 cups)

6 plum tomatoes, quartered

1 oz. Asiago or Parmesan cheese,
  grated (1/4 cup)

1 Cook the sausage meat in a medium saucepan over medium heat, stirring to crumble, until browned. Remove sausage from the pan. Add the cornmeal and pepper to the pan. Gradually add the broth, whisking constantly, and bring to a boil. Reduce the heat to medium and cook, stirring frequently, for 2 minutes. Stir in the sausage and 1 tablespoon of the parsley. Coat a 9-inch pie plate with cooking spray. Spoon the polenta into the plate and spread evenly. Press plastic wrap onto the surface of the polenta. Refrigerate until firm, at least 15 minutes.

2 Preheat the broiler. Coat a baking sheet and a jelly-roll pan with cooking spray.

3 Combine the vinegar, oil, and salt in a medium bowl. Add the mushrooms and tomatoes and toss well. Spread the mushroom-tomato mixture on the jelly-roll pan and broil until the vegetables are soft, about 6 minutes, stirring after 3 minutes. Set aside and keep warm. Cut the polenta into 4 wedges and place on the baking sheet. Broil until lightly browned, about 2 minutes. Transfer to 4 serving plates. Spoon the tomato-mushroom sauce over the polenta. Sprinkle with cheese and the remaining 1 table-spoon parsley and serve.

HEALTH NOTE | *Turkey sausage has half the calories and about half the saturated fat content of regular sausage. Buy it sweet or hot.*

Lamb, Tomato, and White Bean Penne

1 Line a plate with paper towels. Heat the oil in a nonstick sauté pan over medium-high heat and sear the lamb in batches until browned on all sides. Season to taste with salt and pepper. Set aside on the plate.

2 Add the onion to the pan and cook until translucent, about 5 minutes. Add the carrots, celery, and garlic, and cook 2 to 3 minutes more. Add the wine and simmer until reduced by almost half. Add the tomatoes, lamb, beans, sage, and red pepper. Season to taste with salt and pepper.

3 Meanwhile, bring a large pot of water to a boil over high heat. Add the penne and cook until tender. Drain.

4 Simmer the sauce for 10 minutes or until the beans and lamb are heated through, adding water if necessary. Spoon the penne onto 6 plates or into pasta bowls and top with sauce.

TIP | *Treat yourself and use fresh sage if you can—it will make this satisfying dish even tastier.*

SERVES: 6

1 tbsp. olive oil

1 lb. boneless leg of lamb, trimmed of fat and cut into ½-inch cubes

Salt

Freshly ground black pepper

1 onion, finely chopped

2 carrots, finely chopped

2 stalks celery, finely chopped

3 cloves garlic, minced

½ cup dry white wine

1 can (28 oz.) crushed tomatoes

2 cans (15½ oz. each) white beans (cannellini), drained and rinsed

¼ cup chopped fresh sage leaves, or 4 tsp. dried sage

Pinch of crushed red pepper

12 oz. dry penne pasta

CALORIES: **493**   FAT: **9 G**   SAT. FAT: **2 G**   CARBOHYDRATES: **70 G**   PROTEIN: **32 G**   CHOLESTEROL: **50 MG**   SODIUM: **271 MG**   FIBER: **10 G**

ROASTED PORK

HERBS

POTATOES

1 Preheat the oven to 375°.

2 Make several small slits on the outside of the pork and stuff with the garlic slices. Combine the thyme, marjoram, sage, salt, and pepper. Sprinkle the pork with half of the herb mixture. Place the pork in a 13-by-9-inch baking pan.

3 Combine the potatoes, carrots, onion, and oil in a large bowl and sprinkle with the remaining herb mixture. Arrange the vegetable mixture around the pork. Bake for 1 hour 20 minutes or until an instant-read meat thermometer inserted into the thickest portion of the meat registers 160°. Place the pork on a serving platter and cover with aluminum foil. Let stand for 15 minutes before slicing.

TIP | *Infuse the pork with mouth-watering flavors by rubbing seasonings on the outside of the roast and inserting slivers of fresh garlic into the meat.*

SERVES: 8

2 lb. boneless pork loin roast, trimmed of fat

3 cloves garlic, thinly sliced

1¼ tsp. dried thyme

1¼ tsp. dried marjoram

1¼ tsp. dried rubbed sage

½ tsp. salt

½ tsp. freshly ground black pepper

1½ lb. russet baking potatoes, peeled and cubed

1 lb. carrots, peeled and cut into ½-inch pieces

1½ cups coarsely chopped onion

1 tsp. olive oil

CALORIES: 273   FAT: 7 G   SAT. FAT: 2 G   CARBOHYDRATES: 24 G   PROTEIN: 27 G   CHOLESTEROL: 67 MG   SODIUM: 230 MG   FIBER: 4 G

Pork Fillets in Peppery Mushroom Gravy

SERVES: 4

3 cups medium egg noodles

1 pork tenderloin (about 1 lb.)

1 tsp. olive oil

1 cup sliced mushrooms

$\frac{1}{2}$ tsp. minced garlic

1 cup fat-free, reduced-sodium beef broth

2 tbsp. minced sun-dried tomato pieces

1 tbsp. Dijon mustard

1 tbsp. tomato paste

1 tsp. dried thyme

1 tsp. brown sugar

1 tsp. freshly ground black pepper

1 Bring a large pot of water to a boil, add the noodles, and cook as directed on package, until al dente. Drain.

2 While the noodles cook, trim the fat from the pork; cut crosswise into 8 pieces. Place each piece between 2 sheets of heavy-duty plastic wrap and flatten to $\frac{1}{4}$-inch thickness using a meat mallet or rolling pin.

3 Heat the oil in a large nonstick skillet over medium-high heat. Add the pork and sauté for 2 to 3 minutes on each side. Remove from the pan and keep warm. Add the mushrooms and garlic and sauté for 1 minute. Add the broth, sun-dried tomatoes, mustard, tomato paste, thyme, brown sugar, and pepper, and bring to a boil. Cook for 2 minutes, stirring frequently. Return the pork to the skillet, reduce the heat, and simmer for 2 minutes. Serve over the noodles.

HEALTH NOTE | *Avoid pork to protect your heart? There's really no reason to do so. Pork tenderloin is lower in fat than every other red meat, as well as the dark meat of poultry. There's less artery-clogging fat in a serving of this dish than in an ounce of cheese crackers.*

CALORIES: **307**   FAT: **9 G**   SAT. FAT: **3 G**   CARBOHYDRATES: **26 G**   PROTEIN: **29 G**   CHOLESTEROL: **102 MG**   SODIUM: **346 MG**   FIBER: **2 G**

1 Preheat the oven to 400°.

2 Rub the surface of the meat with the oregano, salt, and some pepper. Heat the oil over high heat in a shallow ovenproof casserole. Cook the garlic in the oil for a few seconds, then add the meat and sear it briefly on all sides. Surround the meat with the tomatoes, wine, and lemon juice.

3 Roast, uncovered, turning and basting the meat from time to time with the juices, adding more liquid if necessary. After 1 hour, insert an instant-read meat thermometer into the thickest portion of the roast; the roast is done when it registers 160°.

4 Cover the roast loosely with aluminum foil and let stand for 10 to 15 minutes before slicing. Arrange the slices on a platter and coat with the sauce. If any sauce remains, serve it as an accompaniment.

SERVES: 6

1½ lb. boneless pork loin roast, trimmed of fat, rolled, and tied

1 tbsp. finely chopped fresh oregano, or 1 tsp. dried oregano

1 tsp. salt

Freshly ground black pepper

1 tbsp. extra virgin olive oil

2 cloves garlic, finely chopped

8 oz. plum tomatoes, peeled, seeded, and coarsely chopped

½ cup red wine

2 tbsp. fresh lemon juice

HEALTH NOTE | *Pork is a good source of several B vitamins—thiamin, riboflavin, niacin, and vitamins B_6 and B_{12}—which work with folate to protect your heart.*

CALORIES: **212**   FAT: **11 G**   SAT. FAT: **3 G**   CARBOHYDRATES: **3 G**   PROTEIN: **25 G**   CHOLESTEROL: **70 MG**   SODIUM: **438 MG**   FIBER: **.5 G**

1 Cut the fennel stalks off at the top of the bulb and trim the base of the bulb. Cut the bulb lengthwise into $1/4$-inch slices. You should have about $1 1/2$ cups. Set aside. Chop enough of the fennel fronds to make 1 tablespoon for garnish. Set aside.

2 Trim any fat from the pork and cut crosswise into 8 pieces. Place each piece between 2 sheets of heavy-duty plastic wrap and flatten to $1/2$-inch thickness using a meat mallet or rolling pin. Place the pork pieces and 1 tablespoon of the flour in a large zip-lock plastic bag. Shake to coat.

3 Coat a large nonstick skillet with cooking spray and place over medium heat until hot. Add the pork and cook for 3 minutes on each side until browned. Remove from the skillet and keep warm. Add $1/4$ cup water to the skillet and scrape to loosen any browned bits. Add the sliced fennel, onion, and garlic and sauté for 5 minutes. Add the apple, broth, sage, and thyme. Bring to a boil, cover, reduce the heat, and simmer until the apples are tender, stirring occasionally, about 12 minutes.

4 Combine the remaining 1 tablespoon flour and the milk in a small bowl. Stir with a whisk. Add to the mixture in the skillet. Cook over medium heat until thick, stirring frequently, about 3 minutes. Stir in the lemon juice, mustard, sugar, salt, and pepper. Return the pork to the skillet, cover, and cook over low heat until thoroughly heated, about 3 minutes. Sprinkle with the chopped fennel fronds.

SERVES: 4

1 bulb fennel

1 pork tenderloin (about 1 lb.)

2 tbsp. all-purpose flour

Cooking spray

1 cup thinly sliced onion

2 cloves garlic, minced

1 large Granny Smith apple, thinly sliced

$1/2$ cup fat-free, reduced-sodium chicken broth

$1/2$ tsp. rubbed sage

$1/2$ tsp. dried thyme

1 cup low-fat (1%) milk

2 tsp. fresh lemon juice

$1/2$ tsp. Dijon mustard

$1/2$ tsp. sugar

$1/4$ tsp. salt

$1/8$ tsp. freshly ground black pepper

CALORIES: 241   FAT: 5 G   SAT. FAT: 2 G   CARBOHYDRATES: 21 G   PROTEIN: 28 G   CHOLESTEROL: 76 MG   SODIUM: 365 MG   FIBER: 2 G

Beefy Mushroom and Barley Stew

SERVES: 6

8 oz. beef tenderloin tips, cut into ½-inch pieces

¼ tsp. salt

¼ tsp. freshly ground black pepper

2 tbsp. all-purpose flour

1 tbsp. olive oil

2 tbsp. Worcestershire sauce

1 cup thinly sliced carrots

1 cup chopped shallots

1 clove garlic, minced

8 oz. mushrooms, quartered

1 cup fat-free, reduced-sodium beef broth

1 tsp. dried rosemary, crushed

1 can (14½ oz.) diced tomatoes, with their juices

1 bay leaf

1 cup pearl barley

1 can (14 oz.) quartered artichoke hearts, drained

1 Sprinkle the beef with salt and pepper and dredge in flour. Heat the oil in a large flameproof casserole over medium-high heat, add the beef, and cook for 4 minutes, browning the meat on all sides. Remove from the pot.

2 Reduce the heat to medium, stir in the Worcestershire sauce and 2 tablespoons water, and cook for 1 minute, scraping the pot to loosen any browned bits. Add the carrots, shallots, garlic, and mushrooms, and sauté for 3 minutes.

3 Return the beef to the pot and stir in the broth, rosemary, tomatoes, and bay leaf, and bring to a boil. Add 2½ cups of water, the barley, and artichokes. Bring to a boil, cover, reduce the heat, and simmer for 50 minutes or until the barley is tender. Discard the bay leaf before serving.

HEALTH NOTE | *Barley stews with beef can run high in artery-damaging saturated fat. This recipe uses only a half pound of stew meat, adding plenty of beef flavor while keeping the total and saturated fat amounts down.*

CALORIES: **279**   FAT: **6 G**   SAT. FAT: **1 G**   CARBOHYDRATES: **43 G**   PROTEIN: **15 G**   CHOLESTEROL: **25 MG**   SODIUM: **214 MG**   FIBER: **8 G**

TENDERLOIN

SHALLOTS

ARTICHOKE

SERVES: 4

3 cups fresh parsley leaves

1 tbsp. grated lemon zest

2 cloves garlic

4 beef tenderloin fillets (4 oz. each),
    1 inch thick

½ tsp. salt

¼ tsp. freshly ground black pepper

1 tbsp. olive oil

1 cup dry white wine

1 Place the parsley, lemon zest, and garlic in a food processor and process until minced. Set aside this gremolata.

2 Sprinkle the beef fillets with salt and pepper. Heat the oil over medium-high heat in a large nonstick skillet. Add the fillets and cook 3 minutes on each side or until browned. Remove the steaks from the skillet and keep warm.

3 Stir in the wine, scraping the pan to loosen browned bits. Bring to a boil and cook until reduced, to 2 tablespoons, about 8 minutes. Drizzle the sauce over each steak, sprinkle each with gremolata, and serve.

TIP | *Trim the tenderloin of all visible fat and you will have one of the leanest cuts of beef available.*

Chunky Beef Chili

SERVES: 8

2 dried ancho chili peppers, stemmed, seeded, and quartered

2 jalapeño chili peppers, stemmed, seeded, and coarsely chopped

2 tbsp. canola oil

2 lb. beef chuck, trimmed of fat and cut into ½-inch chunks

2 large onions, finely chopped

2 stalks celery, finely chopped

2 cloves garlic, finely chopped

2 tbsp. finely chopped fresh ginger

1 tbsp. ground cumin

1 tbsp. Mexican oregano

¼ tsp. cayenne

¼ tsp. freshly ground black pepper

1 tbsp. all-purpose flour

1 can (14 oz.) no-salt-added tomatoes, coarsely chopped, with their juices

1 bay leaf

1½ tsp. salt

½ tsp. grated orange zest

1 Put the ancho chilies in a small saucepan, pour in 2 cups of water, and boil for 5 minutes. Turn off the heat and let the chilies soften for 5 minutes.

2 Transfer the chilies to a blender or food processor with ½ cup of their soaking liquid; reserve the remaining liquid. Add the jalapeño chilies and puree until the mixture is very smooth. Strain the puree through a sieve into the reserved soaking liquid, rubbing the solids through with a spoon.

3 Heat ½ tablespoon of the oil over medium-high heat in a large nonstick or heavy-bottomed skillet. Add about one-fourth of the beef chunks and cook them, turning frequently, until browned all over, about 8 minutes. Transfer the browned beef to a large heavy-bottomed pot. Brown the rest of the meat the same way, using all but ½ tablespoon of the remaining oil in the process.

4 Add the last ½ tablespoon of oil to the skillet. Add the onions, celery, and garlic, and sauté for 5 minutes, stirring frequently. Stir in the ginger, cumin, oregano, cayenne, and black pepper, and cook for 1 minute. Add the flour and cook for 1 minute more, stirring constantly. Transfer the mixture to the pot.

5 Pour the reserved chili mixture and 2 cups of water into the pot. Stir in the tomatoes and their juices along with the bay leaf, salt, and orange zest. Cook the mixture, uncovered, over very low heat until the meat is tender, 2½ to 3 hours. (Do not allow the mixture to boil or the meat will toughen.) If the chili begins to get too thick, add water, ½ cup at a time, until it reaches the desired consistency.

CALORIES: **256**   FAT: **13 G**   SAT. FAT: **4 G**   CARBOHYDRATES: **12 G**   PROTEIN: **24 G**   CHOLESTEROL: **74 MG**   SODIUM: **399 MG**   FIBER: **3 G**

Stir-Fried Green Beans

1 Bring 2 quarts of water to a boil in a saucepan over high heat. Squeeze the lime or lemon into the water, then drop in the rind. Add the green beans and cook them for 4 minutes after the water comes back to a boil; they should still be crisp. Drain the beans and refresh them under cold water until cool. Discard the lime rind.

2 Heat the oil in a wok or heavy-bottomed skillet over high heat. Sauté the green beans, stirring constantly, until tender, about 3 minutes. Reduce the heat to medium and cook for 1 minute more. Stir the cornstarch mixture and the black beans together. Pour this mixture onto the green beans, sprinkle with pepper, and stir well. Continue cooking for 1 minute more and transfer to a serving dish. Serve immediately.

SERVES: 6

½ lime or lemon

1 lb. green beans, trimmed

1 tbsp. canola oil

1 tbsp. cornstarch, mixed with 1 tbsp. low-sodium soy sauce and ¼ cup water

2 tbsp. fermented black beans, rinsed

Freshly ground black pepper

NOTE *The fermented black beans called for in this recipe are available in some large supermarkets and wherever Asian foods are sold.*

CALORIES: **49**   FAT: **3 G**   SAT. FAT: **.2 G**   CARBOHYDRATES: **6 G**   PROTEIN: **2 G**   CHOLESTEROL: **0 MG**   SODIUM: **249 MG**   FIBER: **1 G**

Curried Vegetable Couscous

SERVES: 4

2 tsp. olive oil

1 red onion, diced

2 carrots, thinly sliced

2 cloves garlic, minced

2 tsp. curry powder

2 tsp. ground cumin

1 can (14½ oz.) fat-free,
reduced-sodium chicken broth

1 can (15 oz.) chickpeas,
rinsed and drained

¼ cup dried currants or raisins

2 tbsp. mango chutney

1 tbsp. white wine vinegar

2 tsp. grated peeled fresh ginger

½ tsp. salt

¾ cup couscous

3 tbsp. chopped fresh cilantro
or parsley

1 Heat the oil in a large nonstick skillet over medium heat until hot but not smoking. Add the onion and carrots and cook until the onion is translucent, about 5 minutes. Stir in the garlic, curry powder, and cumin and cook for 1 minute to blend the flavors.

2 Add the broth, chickpeas, currants, chutney, vinegar, ginger, and salt and bring to a boil. Remove the skillet from the heat, stir in the couscous, cover, and let stand until the liquid is absorbed, about 5 minutes. Stir in the cilantro and serve.

HEALTH NOTE | *This is a truly well-rounded dish containing vegetables, grain, legumes, and even fruit. Best of all, it's bursting with a variety of great flavors.*

CALORIES: 327   FAT: 5 G   SAT. FAT: .4 G   CARBOHYDRATES: 61 G   PROTEIN: 11 G   CHOLESTEROL: 0 MG   SODIUM: 635 MG   FIBER: 7 G

TOMATOES

LEEKS

MINT

1 Combine the tomato, basil, mint, scallions, salt, lime juice, and olive oil in a bowl and toss gently. Set the salsa aside.

2 Trim away the roots and the dark leaves of the leeks and cut them to 5 inches in length. Halve them lengthwise and place in a bowl of lukewarm water. Let stand for 1 to 2 minutes. Lift the leeks out of the water, leaving the grit behind. Repeat if necessary.

3 Combine the leeks, broth, and basil sprig in a large skillet and bring to a boil. Cover, reduce the heat, and simmer until tender, about 20 minutes. Place the leeks on a platter; discard the poaching liquid. Top the leeks with salsa and pepper and serve.

SERVES: 4

1 cup diced seeded tomato

2 tbsp. coarsely chopped fresh basil

1 tsp. finely chopped fresh mint

1 tbsp. thinly sliced scallions

1/8 tsp. salt

2 tsp. fresh lime juice

2 tsp. olive oil

6 medium leeks

1/2 cup fat-free, reduced-sodium chicken broth

1 sprig of basil

Freshly ground black pepper

CALORIES: **142**   FAT: **3 G**   SAT. FAT: **.5 G**   CARBOHYDRATES: **27 G**   PROTEIN: **3 G**   CHOLESTEROL: **.5 MG**   SODIUM: **126 MG**   FIBER: **3 G**

SERVES: 6

About 3½ lb. butternut squash

1½ tbsp. butter

¼ tsp. salt

1 cup fresh orange juice with pulp

1 tbsp. fresh lime juice

1½ tbsp. grated peeled fresh ginger

1 Cut the squash in half and scrape out the seeds and fibers. Peel the halves and cut them into ½-inch cubes.

2 Melt the butter in a heavy-bottomed skillet over medium heat. Add the squash and sprinkle with the salt. Cook for 20 minutes, stirring and scraping the bottom often. Combine the orange juice, lime juice, and ginger; add to the squash. Continue cooking, stirring frequently, until most of the moisture has evaporated and the mixture has reached a dense, pasty consistency, about 35 minutes.

3 Transfer the squash to a food processor or blender and puree it. Or pass it through a food mill. Spoon the puree into a dish and serve.

HEALTH NOTE | *Butternut squash is one of the most nutritious winter squashes, supplying lots of the antioxidants beta carotene and vitamin C to fight heart disease.*

CALORIES: 146   FAT: 3 G   SAT. FAT: 2 G   CARBOHYDRATES: 31 G   PROTEIN: 3 G   CHOLESTEROL: 8 MG   SODIUM: 105 MG   FIBER: 4 G

1 Combine the sun-dried tomatoes and boiling water in a small bowl and let stand until the tomatoes have softened, about 15 minutes. Drain the tomatoes, reserving ¼ cup of the soaking liquid. Coarsely chop the tomatoes and set aside.

2 Rinse the spinach in lukewarm water and lift it out, leaving the grit behind. Repeat if necessary. Drain.

3 Heat the oil in a large nonstick skillet over medium heat until hot but not smoking. Add the garlic, red pepper, spinach, salt, sugar, and broth; cook until the garlic is fragrant, about 3 minutes. Add the sun-dried tomatoes and the reserved soaking liquid. Cover and cook until the spinach is wilted, about 4 minutes. Spoon onto 4 plates and serve.

HEALTH NOTE | *Spinach is a superstar of the vegetable world, with loads of folate, beta carotene, fiber, and calcium.*

SERVES: 4

½ cup sun-dried tomatoes, not oil-packed

1 cup boiling water

2 lb. fresh spinach leaves

2 tsp. olive oil

2 cloves garlic, minced

⅛ tsp. crushed red pepper

½ tsp. salt

⅛ tsp. sugar

¼ cup fat-free, reduced-sodium chicken broth

CALORIES: 98   FAT: 3 G   SAT. FAT: .4 G   CARBOHYDRATES: 13 G   PROTEIN: 8 G   CHOLESTEROL: 0 MG   SODIUM: 369 MG   FIBER: 8 G

1 Preheat the oven to 400°.

2 Using a melon baller or small spoon, scoop just enough flesh from the zucchini, to leave a ¼-inch-thick shell. Discard the zucchini flesh.

3 Bring 1⅓ cups of water to a boil in a medium saucepan over medium heat. Add the rice and scallions. Reduce the heat to a simmer, cover, and cook until the rice is tender, about 17 minutes. Transfer to a bowl and stir in the beans and ⅓ cup of the salsa.

4 Cut a small slice from the bottom side of each zucchini shell so that it will sit flat. Combine the remaining ⅓ cup of salsa, the tomato sauce, and cilantro in an 11-by-7-inch glass baking dish. Place the zucchini shells on top of the sauce, spoon the rice mixture into the shells and cover with aluminum foil. Bake for about 20 minutes, or until the filling is piping hot and the zucchini shells are tender.

5 Uncover the dish, sprinkle the cheese on top, and bake for about 1 minute or until the cheese is melted. Spoon the sauce over the stuffed zucchini before serving.

SERVES: 4

4 medium zucchini, halved lengthwise

½ cup long-grain rice

4 scallions, thinly sliced

1 can (15 oz.) black beans, rinsed and drained

⅔ cup mild or medium-hot prepared salsa

1 can (8 oz.) no-salt-added tomato sauce

¼ cup chopped fresh cilantro or parsley

1 cup shredded jalapeño jack cheese (4 oz.)

CALORIES: 312   FAT: 10 G   SAT. FAT: 5 G   CARBOHYDRATES: 41 G   PROTEIN: 15 G   CHOLESTEROL: 30 MG   SODIUM: 685 MG   FIBER: 5 G

DESSERTS

SERVES: 16

1 watermelon (about 8 lb.)

1 cup sugar

2½ tbsp. fresh lemon juice

1 cup fresh blueberries

1 Cut the watermelon in half lengthwise. Scoop out all the flesh, removing the seeds in the process.

2 Puree the watermelon flesh in several batches in a blender or food processor. Measure the pureed fruit; you should have about 7 cups. (If you have more or less fruit, increase or decrease the amount of sugar accordingly by 2 tablespoons for each cup of fruit.)

3 Stir the sugar and lemon juice into the pureed fruit.

4 Freeze the mixture in an ice cream maker according to the manufacturer's directions, stirring in the blueberries near the end of the freezing period. (Alternatively, freeze the mixture in a shallow metal cake pan until solid, about 6 hours. Break into chunks and, working in batches, process in a food processor until smooth.)

5 Scoop into dessert cups, garnish with blueberries, and serve.

HEALTH NOTE | *This recipe delivers a double heart benefit: Watermelons, like tomatoes, are rich in the antioxidant lycopene, as well as the mineral potassium, which helps keep blood pressure down; and blueberries are the most powerful of all foods when it comes to mopping up the free radicals implicated in heart disease and cancer. You may mix the blueberries into the sorbet if you prefer.*

CALORIES: 92   FAT: .5 G   SAT. FAT: 0 G   CARBOHYDRATES: 22 G   PROTEIN: .8 G   CHOLESTEROL: 0 MG   SODIUM: 3 MG   FIBER: .7 G

SERVES: 8

5 whole lemons

½ cup sugar

16 citrus leaves or fresh mint leaves (optional)

1 Cut 4 of the lemons in half lengthwise. Remove the pulp and seeds with a melon baller or teaspoon. Place the lemon shells in the freezer. Transfer the pulp to a strainer set over a bowl and press down on the pulp with the back of a wooden spoon to extract all the juice. Discard the pulp and seeds.

2 Wash the fifth lemon well and, using the finest holes on a grater, rub off enough of the deep yellow outer skin to create ½ teaspoon of lemon zest.

3 Strain ½ cup of the lemon juice into a bowl. (Reserve the extra juice for another use.) Stir in 1½ cups water, the sugar, and lemon zest.

4 Freeze the mixture in an ice-cream maker according to the manufacturer's directions. (Alternatively, freeze the mixture in a shallow metal cake pan until solid, about 6 hours. Break into chunks and process in a food processor until smooth.)

5 Spoon the sorbet into the lemon shells and return them to the freezer. Garnish with citrus or mint leaves before serving if desired.

TIP | *If you don't have a grater, you can slice away the outer yellow skin of the lemon with a sharp knife and chop the zest into fine shreds.*

CALORIES: 52   FAT: 0 G   SAT. FAT: 0 G   CARBOHYDRATES: 14 G   PROTEIN: .1 G   CHOLESTEROL: 0 MG   SODIUM: .3 MG   FIBER: .1 G

RICOTTA

BERRIES

MERINGUE

Berry-Filled Meringue Baskets

1 Preheat the oven to 160°. If your oven does not have a setting this low, set it just below 200° and keep the oven door propped open with a ball of crumpled aluminum foil. Line a baking sheet with parchment paper.

2 Put the egg whites and sugar into a large heat-proof bowl. Set the bowl over a pan of simmering water and stir the mixture with a whisk until the sugar has dissolved and the egg whites are hot, about 6 minutes. Remove the bowl from the heat. Using an electric mixer, beat the egg whites on medium-high speed until they form stiff peaks and have cooled to room temperature.

3 Transfer the meringue to a pastry bag fitted with a $\frac{1}{2}$-inch star tip. Holding the tip about $\frac{1}{2}$ inch above the surface of the baking sheet, pipe out the meringue in a tightly coiled spiral to form a flat disk about $3\frac{1}{2}$ inches across. Pipe a single ring of meringue on top of the edge of the disk, forming a low wall that will hold in the filling. Form 7 more meringue baskets the same way.

4 Put the baking sheet into the oven and let the meringues bake for at least 4 hours. The meringues should remain white and be thoroughly dried out. Let the meringues stand at room temperature until cool; they will become quite crisp.

5 Puree the ricotta with the yogurt in a food processor or a blender. Divide the cheese mixture among the meringue baskets, and top each with some of the strawberries and blueberries.

SERVES: 8

3 egg whites

1 cup sugar

$\frac{1}{2}$ cup part-skim ricotta cheese

$\frac{1}{4}$ cup plain low-fat yogurt

2 cups sliced, hulled strawberries

1 cup blueberries, stemmed, picked over, and rinsed

HEALTH NOTE | *The berries in this recipe, packed with fiber and antioxidants, rest on a calcium-rich base of creamy cheese in a light, delicious meringue shell.*

CALORIES: 150   FAT: 2 G   SAT. FAT: .8 G   CARBOHYDRATES: 32 G   PROTEIN: 4 G   CHOLESTEROL: 5 MG   SODIUM: 46 MG   FIBER: 1 G

Mixed Berry Cobbler

SERVES: 8

1 cup old-fashioned rolled oats

¼ cup firmly packed dark
  brown sugar

3 tbsp. butter

2 cups fresh blueberries, picked
  over and stemmed, or 2 cups
  frozen blueberries, thawed

2 cups fresh or frozen
  red raspberries, thawed

2 cups fresh or frozen black
  raspberries or blackberries,
  thawed

¼ cup fresh lemon juice

¼ cup sugar

1 Preheat the oven to 350°.

2 Combine the oats and brown sugar in a small bowl. Spread the mixture
in a baking pan and bake until it turns light brown, 8 to 10 minutes. Cut
the butter into small pieces and scatter them in the pan. Return the pan
to the oven until the butter has melted, about 1 minute. Stir the oats to
coat them with the butter and bake the mixture for 5 minutes more. Set
the oatmeal topping aside to cool. (The topping may be made ahead and
stored, tightly covered, for several days.)

3 Put 1 cup each of the blueberries, the raspberries, and the blackberries in
a 2-quart bowl and set aside. Combine the lemon juice with the sugar in
a saucepan and bring the mixture to a boil. Add the remaining 1 cup of
blueberries to the syrup, reduce the heat to low, and cook for 3 minutes.
Add the remaining 1 cup of raspberries and the remaining 1 cup of blackberries. Bring the mixture to a simmer and cook, stirring constantly, for 3
minutes. Pour the cooked fruit into a sieve set over the bowl of reserved
berries, and use the back of a wooden spoon to press the fruit through
the sieve. Stir gently to coat the whole berries with the sauce.

4 Spoon the warm fruit mixture into individual ramekins or small bowls.
Sprinkle some of the topping over each portion.

HEALTH NOTE | *This cobbler is a good source of potassium, fiber, and
antioxidants from the berries. The topping is buttery and satisfying but keeps
saturated fat in check.*

CALORIES: **183**   FAT: **5 G**   SAT. FAT: **3 G**   CARBOHYDRATES: **34 G**   PROTEIN: **2 G**   CHOLESTEROL: **12 MG**   SODIUM: **6 MG**   FIBER: **5 G**

Plums Poached in Red Wine

SERVES: 4

⅔ cup plain nonfat yogurt

2 tbsp. reduced-fat sour cream

1 cup dry red wine

⅓ cup sugar

1 vanilla bean, split, or ½ tsp. pure
    vanilla extract

2 strips of orange zest
    (3 x ½ inches each)

¼ tsp. ground ginger

6 red or purple plums, halved
    and pitted

1 Combine the yogurt and sour cream in a small bowl. Cover and refrigerate until serving time.

2 Combine the wine, sugar, vanilla bean (if using the vanilla extract, do not add it now), orange zest, and ginger in a medium saucepan. Bring to a boil over medium heat, reduce the heat to simmer, and add the plums, cut side down. Cook, turning once, until the plums are tender, about 12 minutes. Using a slotted spoon, transfer the plums to a shallow bowl and set aside. Return the syrup to the heat and cook, stirring occasionally, until reduced to ½ cup, about 8 minutes. If using the vanilla extract, stir it into the mixture now.

3 Pour the reduced syrup over the plums and cool to room temperature. Refrigerate the plums in the syrup for at least 1 hour or up to 3 days.

4 To serve, remove the orange zest and vanilla bean. Spoon the plums and syrup into 4 dessert bowls and spoon a dollop of the yogurt-sour cream mixture into the bowl.

HEALTH NOTE | *Yogurt is a low-fat, nutrient-rich alternative to whipped topping that goes well with a variety of desserts, such as angel food cake, fruit cobbler, and warm gingerbread.*

CALORIES:**159**   FAT:**2 G**   SAT. FAT:**.6 G**   CARBOHYDRATES:**34 G**   PROTEIN:**4 G**   CHOLESTEROL:**3 MG**   SODIUM:**36 MG**   FIBER:**2 G**

SERVES: 8

Cooking spray

1 lb. nectarines, cut into
$\frac{1}{2}$-inch-thick wedges

1$\frac{1}{3}$ cups firmly packed light
brown sugar

$\frac{1}{4}$ cup cornstarch

1 lb. peaches, cut into
$\frac{1}{2}$-inch-thick wedges

3 tbsp. bourbon, Scotch, or brandy

1 tsp. grated lemon zest

2 tbsp. fresh lemon juice

$\frac{1}{8}$ tsp. ground allspice

$\frac{1}{8}$ tsp. freshly ground black pepper

$\frac{1}{3}$ cup old-fashioned rolled oats

$\frac{1}{3}$ cup all-purpose flour

3 tbsp. butter, cut into small pieces

2 tbsp. reduced-fat sour cream

1 Preheat the oven to 375°. Spray a 6-cup glass or ceramic baking dish with cooking spray.

2 Combine half of the nectarines, 1 cup of the brown sugar, the cornstarch, and 1 tablespoon of water in a medium saucepan. Bring to a boil over medium heat. Remove from the heat and stir in the remaining nectarines, the peaches, bourbon, lemon zest, lemon juice, allspice, and pepper. Pour the mixture into the baking dish.

3 Stir together the oats, flour, and the remaining $\frac{1}{3}$ cup brown sugar in a medium bowl. With a pastry blender or 2 knives, cut in the butter and sour cream until the mixture resembles coarse crumbs. Spread the mixture over the fruit and bake for 30 minutes, or until browned and bubbly. Serve warm or at room temperature.

TIP | *You can use all nectarines or all peaches in this dessert, instead of a mixture, if you like.*

CALORIES: 278   FAT: 5 G   SAT. FAT: 3 G   CARBOHYDRATES: 58 G   PROTEIN: 2 G   CHOLESTEROL: 13 MG   SODIUM: 18 MG   FIBER: 2 G

1 Bring 3 cups of the milk to a boil in a heavy-bottomed saucepan over medium heat. Reduce the heat to low and add the rice, $\frac{1}{4}$ cup of the sugar, and the salt. Cover the mixture and simmer over low heat for 50 minutes, stirring occasionally.

2 Whisk together the egg yolk and $\frac{1}{4}$ cup of the remaining milk in a small saucepan. Whisk in the flour and $\frac{1}{4}$ cup of the remaining sugar, then blend in the remaining $\frac{3}{4}$ cup of milk. Bring the mixture to a boil over medium heat, stirring constantly. Cook it, still stirring vigorously, for 2 minutes more. Remove the pan from the heat and stir in the nutmeg, vanilla, and almond extract.

3 When the rice has finished cooking, stir in the raisins, then fold in the egg mixture. Transfer the pudding to a clean bowl. To prevent a skin from forming, press a sheet of plastic wrap directly onto the pudding. Refrigerate until cold, about 2 hours.

4 Puree the raspberries and the remaining 2 tablespoons of sugar in a blender or a food processor. Rub the puree through a fine sieve with a plastic spatula or the back of a wooden spoon; discard the seeds.

5 Divide the sauce among 8 serving dishes. Top the sauce with individual scoops of pudding. If you like, sprinkle the scoops with some additional nutmeg and garnish each with a sprig of mint.

SERVES: 8

4 cups soy milk or low-fat (1%) milk

$\frac{1}{2}$ cup long-grain rice

$\frac{1}{2}$ cup plus 2 tbsp. sugar

$\frac{1}{4}$ tsp. salt

1 egg yolk

3 tbsp. all-purpose flour

$\frac{1}{2}$ tsp. grated nutmeg

1 tsp. pure vanilla extract

$\frac{1}{4}$ tsp. almond extract

$\frac{1}{4}$ cup golden raisins

2 cups fresh or frozen whole raspberries, thawed

Sprigs of mint (optional)

HEALTH NOTE | *If you use soy milk, you'll be combining cholesterol-lowering soy protein and isoflavones with antioxidant-packed berries to make this super heart-healthy.*

CALORIES:**193** FAT:**3 G** SAT. FAT:**0 G** CARBOHYDRATES:**37 G** PROTEIN:**5 G** CHOLESTEROL:**26 MG** SODIUM:**88 MG** FIBER:**3 G**

Pears with Hazelnuts

SERVES: 4

¼ cup hazelnuts (about 1 oz.)

¼ cup firmly packed light
   brown sugar

1 tbsp. cold unsalted butter

4 large ripe pears

½ lemon

1 tbsp. fresh lemon juice

1 Preheat the oven to 375°.

2 Spread the hazelnuts in a single layer in a small cake pan or roasting pan. Toast the nuts for 10 minutes. Test a nut for doneness by rubbing it in a clean kitchen towel; the skin should come off easily. If not, toast the nuts for 2 minutes more and repeat the test. When the nuts are done, wrap them in the towel and rub off their skins. Let the nuts cool to room temperature.

3 Put the nuts, brown sugar, and butter in a food processor or blender and process just until the nuts are coarsely chopped. Set aside.

4 Preheat the broiler. Peel the pears, halve them lengthwise, and core them, rubbing with the lemon half as you work to prevent discoloration. Arrange the pear halves, cored side up, in a large, shallow baking dish. Moisten the pears with the lemon juice and sprinkle the nut mixture over them. Broil until the topping browns and bubbles, about 2 minutes.

HEALTH NOTE | *Many studies show that cholesterol levels drop when nuts are added to the diet. They are high in calories, though, so be careful.*

CALORIES: 246   FAT: 8 G   SAT. FAT: 2 G   CARBOHYDRATES: 46 G   PROTEIN: 2 G   CHOLESTEROL: 8 MG   SODIUM: 6 MG   FIBER: 6 G

BROWN SUGAR

PEARS

HAZELNUTS

1 In a 3-to 4-quart wide shallow pan, combine 3 cups of water with the wine, sugar, cinnamon, and 1 tablespoon of the orange zest. Bring to a boil over high heat, cover, and simmer for 15 minutes. Add the pears, cover, and simmer until Asian pears are crisp-tender when pierced or regular pears are very tender, 15 to 25 minutes, turning the fruit over occasionally. Using a slotted spoon, remove the pears and set aside. If you are making them ahead, cover and refrigerate for up to 1 day. Discard the cinnamon sticks.

2 Boil the liquid in the pan, uncovered, over high heat until reduced to ³/₄ cup, about 20 minutes. Remove from the heat and stir in the chocolate and vanilla; the mixture will look separated. Let stand until slightly cool, at least 5 minutes, then whisk to blend the chocolate in smoothly. Serve hot, warm, or cold. If making ahead, cover and refrigerate for up to 1 day.

3 Arrange the pear halves on 4 plates and pour the chocolate sauce over and around the fruit. Sprinkle with the remaining orange zest and garnish with mint.

NOTE | *Delicious Asian pears are round and very crisp; they are now found in most supermarkets, but if they are not available, you can substitute Bosc pears instead.*

SERVES: 4

1¹/₂ cups dessert wine

¹/₂ cup sugar

2 sticks cinnamon, each about 3 inches long

About 1¹/₂ tbsp. orange zest

4 Asian or other firm ripe pears, each about 8 oz., peeled, halved lengthwise, and cored

1 oz. unsweetened chocolate, chopped

1 tsp. pure vanilla extract

Sprigs of mint, for garnish

CALORIES: 264   FAT: 4 G   SAT. FAT: 2 G   CARBOHYDRATES: 59 G   PROTEIN: 2 G   CHOLESTEROL: 0 MG   SODIUM: 10 MG   FIBER: 8 G

Apple-Cranberry Crisp

SERVES: 6

Cooking spray

4 Granny Smith apples, cored
   and cut into 8 wedges

½ cup dried cranberries

3 tbsp. apple juice

¼ cup all-purpose flour

¼ cup old-fashioned rolled oats

⅓ cup firmly packed brown sugar

¾ tsp. ground cinnamon

¼ tsp. ground nutmeg

1½ tbsp. cold butter, cut
   into small pieces

1 Preheat the oven to 375°. Coat an 8-inch square baking dish with cooking spray.

2 Combine the apples, cranberries, and apple juice in a bowl, toss well, and set aside. Combine the flour, rolled oats, brown sugar, cinnamon, and nutmeg in another bowl. Cut in the butter with a pastry blender until the mixture resembles coarse meal. Transfer the apple mixture to the baking dish and sprinkle evenly with the flour mixture. Lightly coat the top with cooking spray.

3 Cover and bake for 30 minutes. Uncover and bake for 20 minutes more, or until the apples are tender. Let stand for at least 20 minutes before serving.

TIP | *If you want to increase the fiber content of this dessert, use whole-wheat flour. Apples are high in pectin—a type of soluble fiber shown to lower cholesterol levels, and the oat topping provides additional soluble fiber.*

CALORIES: **193**   FAT: **4 G**   SAT. FAT: **2 G**   CARBOHYDRATES: **40 G**   PROTEIN: **1 G**   CHOLESTEROL: **8 MG**   SODIUM: **35 MG**   FIBER: **3 G**

MAPLE SYRUP

PINEAPPLE

GOLDEN RAISINS

1 Trim and peel the pineapple. Stand the pineapple upright and cut it in half from top to bottom. Remove the core from each half by cutting a shallow V-shaped groove down the center, then cut each half crosswise into 9 slices.

2 Preheat the oven to 500°.

3 Overlap the pineapple slices in a large shallow baking dish. Scatter the dark raisins and golden raisins over the pineapple slices. Drizzle 2 tablespoons of the maple syrup over the top, then sprinkle the dish with 2 tablespoons of the bourbon. Cover the dish and set it aside at room temperature.

4 In a small bowl, blend the egg yolk with the vanilla, ginger, cornstarch, the remaining 3 tablespoons of maple syrup, and the remaining 1 tablespoon of bourbon. In a separate bowl, beat the egg whites until they form soft peaks. Stir half of the beaten egg whites into the yolk mixture to lighten it. Gently fold the yolk mixture into the remaining beaten egg whites.

5 Bake the pineapple until the slices are heated through, about 3 minutes. Remove the dish from the oven and spread the egg mixture evenly over the fruit. Rub the sugar through a sieve over the top of the egg mixture. Return the dish to the oven and bake until the sugar melts and the topping browns and puffs up slightly, about 5 minutes. Serve the gratin immediately.

SERVES: 6

1 large ripe pineapple

2 tbsp. dark raisins

2 tbsp. golden raisins

5 tbsp. pure maple syrup

3 tbsp. bourbon or white rum

1 egg yolk

½ tsp. pure vanilla extract

¼ tsp. ground ginger

1 tbsp. cornstarch

2 egg whites, at room temperature

2 tbsp. dark brown sugar

CALORIES: 195   FAT: 2 G   SAT. FAT: .3 G   CARBOHYDRATES: 41 G   PROTEIN: 2 G   CHOLESTEROL: 35 MG   SODIUM: 25 MG   FIBER: 2 G

Winter Fruit Compote

SERVES: 6

½ cup sugar

1-inch piece fresh ginger, peeled
and very thinly slivered

2 Granny Smith apples, peeled,
cored, and cut into wedges

1 firm-ripe pear, peeled, cored,
and cut into ¾-inch chunks

½ cup dried apricots

2 cups fresh or frozen cranberries

2 oranges, peeled and sectioned

1 Combine the sugar, 1½ cups of water, and the ginger in a large saucepan. Bring to a boil over high heat. Add the apples, pear, and apricots. Reduce the heat to low and simmer, uncovered, until the fruit is softened, about 5 minutes.

2 Add the cranberries and cook, stirring occasionally, until the cranberries pop, about 5 minutes. Stir in the orange sections and remove from the heat. Transfer the compote to a bowl and serve warm or at room temperature.

HEALTH NOTE | *This dessert is a heart protection powerhouse: Fiber from the pears, apples, and apricots combines with antioxidants from the cranberries and the oranges.*

CALORIES:**173**   FAT:**.5 G**   SAT. FAT:**0 G**   CARBOHYDRATES:**44 G**   PROTEIN:**1 G**   CHOLESTEROL:**0 MG**   SODIUM:**2 MG**   FIBER:**5 G**

ALLSPICE

BEAUJOLAIS

CURRANTS

1 With a vegetable peeler, remove the zest from one of the oranges. Put the zest into a small saucepan with the wine, sugar, cinnamon stick, and cardamom. Bring to a boil and cook over medium-high heat until the liquid is reduced to about $^2/_3$ cup, about 5 minutes. Remove the pan from the heat, stir in the port and currants, and set aside.

2 Cut away the skins, removing all the white pith, and slice the oranges into $^1/_4$-inch-thick rounds. Arrange the orange rounds on a serving dish and pour the wine sauce over them. Remove and discard the cinnamon stick. Refrigerate the dish, covered, for 2 hours.

3 Just before serving the oranges, sprinkle the toasted coconut over all.

HEALTH NOTE | *This vitamin C-rich dessert is packed with artery-protecting antioxidants contributed by the red wine and the port.*

SERVES: 8

6 large navel oranges

1 cup Beaujolais or other red wine

$^1/_4$ cup sugar

1 cinnamon stick, about 3 inches

$^1/_8$ tsp. ground cardamom or allspice

$^1/_3$ cup ruby port wine

2 tbsp. dried currants

2 tbsp. sweetened coconut, toasted at 325° for 5 minutes

CALORIES: 114   FAT: .5 G   SAT. FAT: .3 G   CARBOHYDRATES: 25 G   PROTEIN: 2 G   CHOLESTEROL: 0 MG   SODIUM: 7 MG   FIBER: 3 G

Metric Conversions

DRY/SOLID INGREDIENT EQUIVALENTS

	U.S.	METRIC
Baking powder/soda	1 tsp	3 gm
Butter	8 tbsp = 1/2 cup = 4 oz	125 gm
Cheese, grated	1 cup = 4 oz	120 gm
Cornmeal	1 cup	150 gm
Cornstarch	1/4 cup	30 gm
Flour		
All-purpose, unsifted	1 cup	120 gm
Cake or pastry, sifted	1 cup	100 gm
Whole-wheat, unsifted	1 cup	125 gm
Nuts, coarsely chopped	1 cup	140 gm
Herbs, dry	1 tsp	2 gm
Rice, uncooked	1 cup	150 gm
Salt	1 tsp	5 gm
Spices, ground	1 tsp	2 gm
Sugar		
Granulated	1 tsp	5 gm
	1 tbsp	15 gm
	1 cup	200 gm
Confectioners'	1 cup	110 gm
Brown, packed	1 cup	220 gm

LIQUID/VOLUME MEASURES

U.S.	METRIC
1 tsp	5 ml
1 tbsp (1/2 fl oz)	15 ml
1/4 cup (2 fl oz)	60 ml
1/3 cup	80 ml
1/2 cup (4 fl oz)	125 ml
2/3 cup	160 ml
3/4 cup (6 fl oz)	185 ml
1 cup (8 fl oz)	250 ml
1 quart (32 fl oz)	950 ml

WEIGHTS

U.S.	METRIC
1 oz	30 gm
1 lb	450 gm
22 lb	1 kg

LINEAR MEASUREMENTS

U.S.	METRIC
1/4 in	.75 cm
1/2 in	1.5 cm
3/4 in	2 cm
1 in	2.5 cm

OVEN TEMPERATURES

°FAHRENHEIT	°CELSIUS
250 (low oven)	120
300	150
325	160
350 (moderate oven)	175
400	200
425 (hot oven)	220
450	230
500 (very hot oven)	260